THE PHILIPPINES

THE MOST BEAUTIFUL PLACES

THE PHILIPPINES

THE MOST BEAUTIFUL PLACES

Nigel Hicks

JOHN BEAUFOY PUBLISHING

Page 1: Paliton Beach, on Siquijor Island, in the Visayas.

Previous page: Sunrise at Pagudpud, in Luzon, close to the northernmost tip of the Philippines' mainland.

Right: A Philippine tropical island retreat; the shore of Pandan Island, in Honda Bay, off the east coast of Palawan.

First published in the United Kingdom in 2014 by John Beaufoy Publishing,
11 Blenheim Court, 316 Woodstock Road, Oxford OX2 7NS, England
www.johnbeaufoy.com

10 9 8 7 6 5 4 3 2 1

ISBN 978-1-909612-16-7

Editor: Krystyna Mayer
Designer: Nimbus Design
Project manager: Rosemary Wilkinson

Printed and bound in Malaysia by Times Offset (M) Sdn. Bhd.

Contents

Clockwise from top left: Plantation Bay Resort, Mactan Is, Cebu;
Manila Bay; Taal Volcano; El Nido, Palawan; Katibawasan Falls,
Camiguin Is, Mindanao; Dumaguete, Negros; Chocolate Hills, Bohol,
The Visayas; Lagen Is, El Nido, Palawan; Miagao Church, near Iloilo,
Panay; Rice terraces at Batad, Luzon; El Nido, Palawan; Corella church,
Corella, Bohol; Farmland around Rawis, near Legazpi, Luzon.

Introduction

With its rugged volcanic mountain landscapes, rich farmlands, dazzlingly white sand beaches and stunning submarine coral reefs, the Philippines is one vast, three-dimensional canvas painted by nature. It is harsh, soft, homely and comfortable, yet sometimes a little threatening and challenging. Much of it is infused with a palette of rich vibrant greens and startlingly powerful blues. These, without any doubt, are the signature colours of the Philippines' physical landscape.

Scattered among it all are the cities, towns and villages that form the setting for much of the Philippines' human landscape, which is bustling and crowded, noisy and colourful, and almost always friendly and welcoming. Etched into this human scene are the history and culture of these islands, from early human migrations and intermingling, through religious and social beliefs and customs, to art and construction. The millennia-long movements of people in this area are reflected in the myriad faces of people walking the streets, and working the fields and boats. Art and construction are visible in the historic Spanish-era churches and museums. Religion and social beliefs, though obvious to a Filipino, are perhaps initially difficult to spot by the outside observer. However, they form an essential and integral everyday part of the multi-coloured Philippine fabric.

Woven together, all these factors make for a fascinating country, and when mixed together in just the right ways they help to generate its most beautiful places. Their beauty may not lie only in their physical appearance, but in the society and culture too, making for a heady concoction that creates a place which feels wonderful to be in, even though you may not be able to pinpoint exactly why.

FROM CORAL REEF TO MOUNTAIN SUMMIT

With the Philippines scattered across more than 7,000 islands, it is not surprising that coastal scenery figures prominently in the list of the country's most important landscapes. It is a fact further compounded by the relative inaccessibility of many inland areas, most of which are quite mountainous, coupled with those areas' appallingly high rainfall, making them difficult or undesirable to either visit or indeed live in.

Top right: In the shade of a Flame of the Forest Tree, on Rizal Boulevard in central Puerto Princesa, Palawan.

Centre right: The village of Guimbitayan, on Malapascua Island, Cebu.

Bottom right: A church of the Iglesia ni Cristo sect, in Puerto Princesa, Palawan.

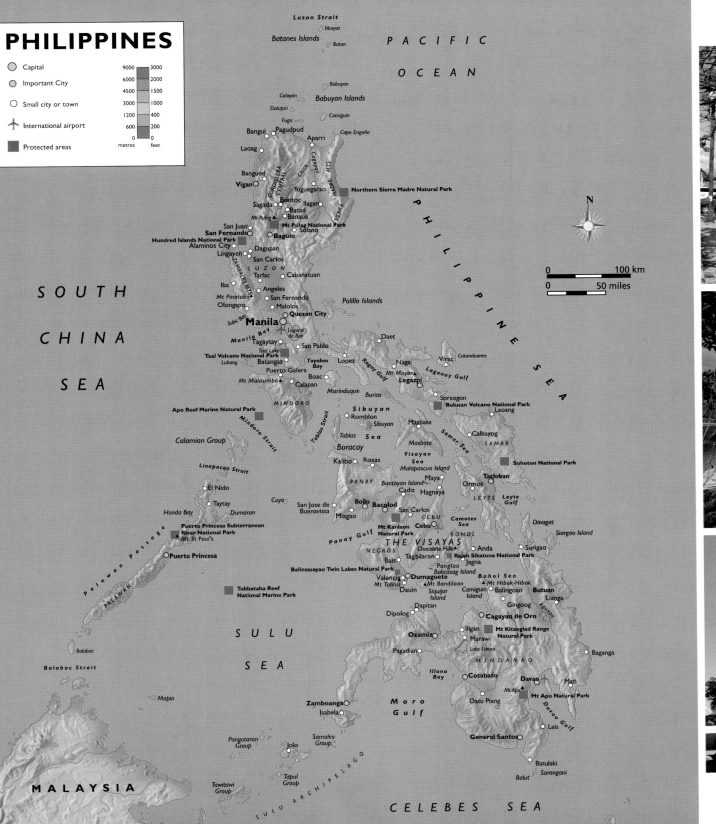

PHILIPPINES

PACIFIC OCEAN

PHILIPPINE SEA

SOUTH CHINA SEA

SULU SEA

CELEBES SEA

MALAYSIA

Luzon Strait

Batanes Islands
Itbayat
Baton

Babuyan Islands
Calayan
Dalupiri
Fuga
Babuyan
Camiguin
Cape Engaño

Bangui
Pagudpud
Aparri
Laoag
Bangued
Vigan
Tuguegarao
Sagada
Bontoc
Ilagan
Batad
Mt Pulag
Banaue
San Juan
Solano
San Fernando
Baguio
Mt Pulag National Park
Hundred Islands National Park
Alaminos City
Dagupan
Lingayen
San Carlos
Iba
Cabanatuan
Tarlac
Angeles
Mt Pinatubo
San Fernando
Olongapo
Malolos
Quezon City
Subic Bay
Manila
Laguna de Bay
Manila Bay
Tagaytay
San Pablo
Daet
Taal Lake
Lubang
Batangas
Lopez
Naga
Virac
Catanduanes
Puerto Galera
Boac
Mt Mayon
Legazpi
Mt Malasimbo
Calapan
Sorsogon
Bulusan Volcano National Park
Marinduque
Burias
Laoang
MINDORO
Apo Reef Marine Natural Park
Sibuyan
Calbayog
Romblon
Masbate
SAMAR
Sibuyan
Calamian Group
Tablas
Masbate
Samar Sea
Sea
Mindoro Strait
Boracay
Visayan Sea
Sohoton National Park
Linapacan Strait
Kalibo
Roxas
Malapascua Island
Tacloban
El Nido
PANAY
Maya
Ormoc
LEYTE
Leyte Gulf
Taytay
Cuyo
Bantayan Island
Cadiz
Hagnaya
Dumaran
San Jose de Buenavista
Iloilo
Bacolod
San Carlos
Honda Bay
Miagao
CEBU
Camotes Sea
Dinagat
Puerto Princesa Subterranean River National Park
Mt St Paul's
Mt Kanlaon Natural Park
Cebu
BOHOL
Siargao Island
Puerto Princesa
Chocolate Hills
Anda
Surigao
THE VISAYAS
Rajah Sikatuna National Park
Jagna
NEGROS
Bais
Tagbilaran
Balinsasayao Twin Lakes Natural Park
Valencia
Dumaguete
Panglao
Balicasag Island
Bohol Sea
Mt Talinis
Dauin
Mt Bandilaan
Butuan
Tubbataha Reef National Marine Park
Siquijor Island
Camiguin Island
Balingoan
Lianga
Gingoog
Dapitan
Dipolog
Cagayan de Oro
Iligan
Mt Kitanglad Range Natural Park
Ozamiz
Marawi
Baganga
Pagadian
Lake Lanao
MINDANAO
Balabac
Balabac Strait
Mapin
Illana Bay
Cotabato
Davao
Mati
Mt Apo
Mt Apo Natural Park
Datu Piang
Zamboanga
Moro Gulf
Isabela
Davao Gulf
Lais
Pangutaran Group
Samales Group
General Santos
Jolo
Tapul Group
Batulaki
Sarangani
Balut
SULU ARCHIPELAGO
Tawitawi Group

CORDILLERA CENTRAL
Cagayan
Chico
SIERRA MADRE MTS
ZAMBALES MTS
LUZON
Northern Sierra Madre Natural Park
Polillo Islands
Ragay Gulf
Tayabas Bay
Lagonoy Gulf
Tablas Strait
Panay Gulf
Aguan

N

0		100 km
0		50 miles

The coastal splendour begins beneath the waves with the thousands of coral reefs that line, protect and nurture many of the Philippines' coastlines. So important are the country's reefs that global conservation organisations have included the entire Philippine coast in the 'Coral Triangle', a region of the western Pacific that has been identified as vital to the continued health of marine ecosystems throughout much of the tropics.

Millions of years of constant reef building and destruction have generated the magnificent white-sand beaches that line many of the Philippines' coasts. They are usually backed either naturally by tropical forest, or – through farming – by lines of the ubiquitous coconut palm. The result is the quintessential tropical paradise beach, sought after by beach-lovers the world over.

The coast quickly gives way to farmland, usually comprising either immense stretches of coconut palms or sugar cane, or a patchwork of rice fields and fruit trees (from bananas to mangoes and much more). As the land climbs into what is mostly a very mountainous interior, the farmland slowly gives way to natural forest. This initially consists of rather damaged and disturbed patches of lowland forest (sadly often in retreat), then higher up of dense, tangled stands of rain- and fog-soaked montane and mossy forests.

Above all this stand the mountain peaks, some submerged beneath the intertwined tentacles of a mossy forest, others standing clear and grass covered. Among these forests and mountains are scattered the Philippines' volcanoes, many of which are topped by gaping, menacing craters. Most are presently inactive, but some (22 at the latest count) are still active, their craters scarred and devoid of vegetation, here and there smouldering ominously.

THE HUMAN LANDSCAPE

Nowhere in the Philippines is completely without human influence, an input that provides some crucial defining feature which either works against and marrs the natural landscape, or works in harmony with it and helps to crystallise its beauty. In short, many of the most lovely places are the result of a collaboration (deliberate or accidental) between the human and natural worlds, and this is the essential nature of many of the places described in this book. A few, however, concentrate largely on the human

Left: A view of Lake Balinsasayao, Balinsasayao Twin Lakes Natural Park, near Dumaguete, Negros.

environment, focusing on achievements in the urban landscape such as historic churches and museums, religious and social practices, arts and crafts, and even commercial activities. They are all part of what makes the Philippines an extraordinary and exciting place to explore.

GETTING AROUND THE PHILIPPINES

One essential ingredient in enjoying any exploration of the Philippines is the journey involved; the process of getting from one place to the next. Getting around is not difficult – it is actually quite straightforward – but the travelling should always be viewed as part of the adventure, rather than being regarded as a chore to be borne between locations.

Travel in the Philippines is rarely dull, if only because on one day you can find yourself taking virtually every form of transport known to humankind. You could, for example, start off with a colourful tricycle, then move on to an equally colourful and even noisier

boat (usually the classic Philippine *banca*, a narrow boat balanced by huge bamboo outriggers). After that you might take a bus (generally including entertainment in the form of very loud 1970's rock music), then an aircraft, and finally either a taxi or another tricycle.

Accommodation, too, is nearly always easily available, with styles and budgets to suit almost every taste and wallet, from simple lodges through to five-star international resorts, the former usually run by a local family, the latter of course generally by a major corporation.

Almost regardless of the transport or the type of accommodation, in the Philippines any travellers can be pretty certain that they will be welcomed and helped along their way by unbelievably accommodating, friendly and unhurried people, who often simply cannot do enough to help make the trip a success.

Right: The façade of Miagao Church, a UNESCO World Heritage Site, in the town of Miagao, near Iloilo, Panay.

Luzon

Luzon is the Philippines' largest and most populous island, site of Manila, the nation's capital, centre for much of its industry and home to Tagalog, the most widely spoken of the many diverse Filipino languages. Despite this, Luzon is not just a conglomeration of towns and cities, but in fact contains a myriad wild and beautiful landscapes, from surf-bound beaches to rugged, forest-clad volcanoes and mountains. Those presented here range from the beaches of Pagudpud in the far north, to the highly active Taal Volcano in the south, passing by the lovely Hundred Islands National Park on the west coast and the peaceful, forested mountain retreat of Sagada in between.

Cultural and historical sites lie scattered across this landscape, starting with those in Manila, and reaching out to the well-preserved, colonial Hispanic town of Vigan on the north-west coast and the stunning ancient rice terraces around Banaue in the mountains, both now UNESCO World Heritage Sites.

The lush emerald green rice terraces around Batad, a World Heritage Site in the Cordillera Central mountains of northern Luzon.

Pagudpud

Right: A local boy gets a ride on Blue Lagoon's surf.

Centre right: Shortly after dawn, the hills and cliffs around Pagudpud lie bathed in mist and motionless cloud.

Far right: Sunrise over the Dos Hermanos Islands, just off Blue Lagoon.

Below right: On a calm morning, a small fishing *banca* lies drawn up on the sand of Blue Lagoon beach.

Above: Early morning sunlight shimmers across the waters of Pagudpud's Blue Lagoon, silhouetting a coconut palm.

Sitting close to the northernmost tip of Luzon's mainland, until recently this remote place was well off any beaten track. However, Pagudpud's two stunningly white sandy beaches, Saud and Blue Lagoon, have started to attract increasing numbers of people, led by surfers drawn by the latter's waves.

BLUE LAGOON BEACH

At Blue Lagoon white surf rolls in across an azure sea, roaring up to a crescent-shaped white-sand shore, backed by dense coconut groves and hemmed in by steep, verdant mountains, the tops permanently lost (or so it seems) in threatening thunderous clouds. The waves are at their best for surfers during the south-west monsoon season (July to September), whereas the onshore winds of the north-east monsoon (October to April or May) frequently break up the wave patterns into an inconsistent chop but provide great conditions for windsurfing and kite-surfing.

At the forefront of the surfing scene – and largely responsible for getting it started at Pagudpud – sits Kapuluan Vista Resort, one of Blue Lagoon's longest established resorts, located not beside Blue Lagoon Beach itself, but a 10-minute walk beyond, through coconut groves and on its own personal piece of sandy shore. Right here, just off this little beach, is what surfers consider to be just about Pagudpud's best surfing break.

For those less concerned about the surfing, the spot is also fantastically picturesque, as a few hundred metres offshore sit the twin islands of Dos Hermanos, conveniently placed to create the almost perfect sunrise silhouette. Turn your back on those islands and in either direction along the mainland shore are fantastic views of beach and rocky shorelines backed by those high, glowering mountains – absolutely stunning in the golden sunlight that prevails for a short time after sunrise.

The crescent-shaped bay in which the main Blue Lagoon Beach nestles is the principal attraction for non-surfers. It is reached from the Laoag-to-Claveria coastal road via a long, bumpy and sometimes steep track. The journey there is worth the effort, however, as this is a truly beautiful place, an arc of blinding golden sand cutting between deep blue sea and intensely green vegetation. A steadily growing number of resorts is attracting more people, of course, but the ambience remains laid-back and peaceful. The main activities on offer for those not into exertion on the water involving simply stretching out on the sand or splashing around in the surf and generally soaking up the sun.

» SAUD BEACH

About 16 km (10 miles) west of Blue Lagoon is Saud Beach, for the past few years the main heart of Pagudpud's non-surfing beach scene, and the centre of the majority of the area's resorts. Saud is a very different place from Blue Lagoon. A vast white sandy beach stretches for several kilometres along the coast. It is a remarkably wide (as well as immensely long) expanse of sand backed by the usual coconut palms, but not hemmed in by any rugged mountains and therefore yielding a relatively open vista. It is a less scenic landscape, perhaps, than that at Blue Lagoon, but also less rugged and wild.

The sea is much calmer here, too. The beach lies at the eastern end of Bangui Bay and is protected from the Pacific swells and surf by Mayraira Point, a short distance to the north. As a result Saud is an easy and relaxing place for those who want to swim or simply loll about and lie in the gently rocking, cooling water, free from concerns about the potential power of the next wave.

Right and far right: Pagudpud's Saud beach is renowned for its hugely long stretch of golden sand, backed by the ubiquitous coconut palm.

» EXPLORING FURTHER

Heading eastwards from Blue Lagoon brings you eventually to Pagudpud's least visited beach, Pannzian (sometimes written Pansian), on the shores of Pasaleng Bay. Although it is a vast beach, it suffers in competition with Blue Lagoon and Saud due to its coarse grey sand and often rather turbulent waters. For those who really want to get away from it all and chill out for a while, however, this would be the place to head for.

Beyond the sand and surf there are a number of mostly inland places to explore, starting with – strictly for the most energetic – a host of hiking and mountain-biking trails in the hills behind Blue Lagoon. Rather gentler is the walk to Kabigan Falls, a 30-minute stroll from the nearby road head through rice fields, into forest, then up a short distance at the base of the inland mountain range. It is a picturesque

site – the waterfall cascades down a sheer cliff straight into a natural pool shaded by the forest crowding around it, making it a popular swimming spot with locals and visitors alike.

Heading back along the coast road towards Laoag you come to the town of Bangui and the western rim of Bangui Bay, site of a long, sweeping line of huge modern wind turbines forming an arc along the edge of the pebbly shore. They are quite a spectacular sight that may not be to everyone's taste but, perhaps due to the contrast between the technology and the landscape, are rapidly becoming a big visitor attraction. The beach along which they stand is now complete with souvenir stands selling – of course – model windmills. The windmills are real behemoths of 21st-century futuristic (hopefully sustainable) technology, a surprising sight in this otherwise quiet and undeveloped part of the country.

Left: The lovely Kabigan Falls cascade down a cliff on the edge of forested hills that climb up into the mountains of northern Luzon.

Above: The path to the falls passes through verdant rice fields, the forested hills looming in the background.

21

Right: A group of *calesas*, or horse-drawn carriages, wait for passengers outside the cathedral. They are a popular form of taxi, particularly in the motor vehicle-free areas of the historic Mestizo district.

Below: The beautiful façade, plus the separate belfry, of the 18th century St Paul's Cathedral, a showpiece of the Vigan World Heritage Site.

Vigan

Above: A statue of a mounted St Paul, set into the façade of St Paul's Cathedral.

The city of Vigan, lying on Luzon's north-west coast, is home to what is without doubt the Philippines' most well-preserved historical relic: the streets of its traditional old Mestizo district, as well as the nearby St Paul's Cathedral, a throwback to Spanish colonial times. In a country whose earliest buildings were largely made of wood and were consequently lost long ago, and whose more recent stone structures were ravaged by the Second World War, Vigan represents a rare opportunity to step back into the Philippines' history, at least as far as the Spanish period of the 17th to 19th centuries.

The Spanish settlement was founded in the 1570s by Juan de Salcedo, to extend Spanish control into the north. Vigan has been around a lot longer than that, having been an important trading post with China and Southeast Asia for many years, but it was with the arrival of the Spanish in 1572 that the build-up of the relics we see today began, starting with the 18th-century St Paul's Cathedral and culminating with the largely 19th-century Mestizo district.

THE HISTORICAL AREA

Since being declared a UNESCO World Heritage Site in 1999, many of the Mestizo district's old buildings, which had been slowly crumbling towards ruination, have been sensitively restored, and the area is now a bustling scene of shops, cafes and souvenir stalls.

Calle Crisologo, the main street, is especially busy with visitors and forms the focus of the area.

The Mestizo district is perfused with a relaxed, easy-going mood, even when it is busy, something that is at least in part due to a ban on motorized traffic from Crisologo. Traditional horse-drawn carriages, known as *calesa*, are the only form of transportation allowed here. They perfectly complement the historical mood of these streets, and provide a relaxed taxi service running mainly between Crisologo and Plaza Salcedo, just outside the cathedral.

Sitting at the eastern end of the plaza, St Paul's Cathedral is a beautifully restored structure, built right at the end of the 18th century (it was finally completed in 1800) on the site of at least two earlier churches. It is in what is called 'Earthquake Baroque' style, meaning that, although its general architecture is in the Baroque style that was typical of southern Europe at the time, its walls were also massively strengthened to enable it to resist both earthquakes and attacks. That strengthening has enabled St Paul's Cathedral to survive unscathed to the present day, its lovely yellow façade complemented perfectly inside by the simplicity of its whitewashed walls and columns – during the day a cool and refreshing escape from the heat outside.

» The Mestizo district starts a little to the south, beyond Plaza Burgos, the north–south Calle Crisologo drawing you in like a magnet. Its lines of souvenir and antiques stalls, though interesting in themselves, can be a little distracting for those wanting to enjoy the historic architecture, so it is a good idea to explore some of the quieter side streets. They are less likely to be the centre of any 'action' – if there is anything like that anyway – but contain a number of well-restored villas. Some, such as the atmospheric 18th-century Villa Angela, now serve as hotels, while others (including the Syquia Mansion) are museums dedicated to the history of life and culture in Vigan.

The buildings that line the neat grid of streets are almost universally two-storied, largely brick and/or stone structures (though the upper floors are sometimes wooden) covered with crumbling white or yellow plaster. The strong Hispanic influence is immediately striking, a mix of historic Spanish and Mexican styles, though there are also inputs from Chinese, Southeast Asian and native Filipino tastes. Perhaps the most visible sign of the last is in the windows, which are frequently light, sliding screens filled with translucent capiz shells rather than glass, a very simple yet also highly attractive feature.

Inside the museums and hotel villas you are treated to a plethora of antique furniture, from dining tables to beds and harps, often in strong Hispanic styles. Many of these items were imported from Mexico and during the Spanish era were in high demand among Vigan's elite.

Right: Detail of a frieze of the Virgin Mary, set into a wall on Calle Crisologo.

Far right: A view of Hispanic buildings lining Calle Crisologo, the main street through the Mestizo district, and centrepiece of the World Heritage Site.

Above: In Vigan, even the tricycles are a bit special, as seen in this detail of the metal canopy typical of the city's three-wheeled taxis.

Left: A terrace garden at the Syquia Mansion, one of the historic homes opened up as a museum to both the city and the wealthy famlies that lived here.

» THE MODERN CITY

Even the modern city largely surrounding the Mestizo district seems to be infused with at least a little of the historical area's ambience. Alhough the streets are crowded with the usual motorbikes, tricycles and *jeepneys* (small buses), the general atmosphere is relaxed and friendly, and the typical harshness of many of the urban streets is softened by trees. This is particularly the case around the central Plazas Burgos and Salcedo; the former is lined with food stalls, while the latter is a lake-filled park that in the evenings is often the site of musical fountain displays.

A civic pride and quiet confidence pervade the city's air, something that is reflected even in the hordes of tricycles. Each of them has a special, uniquely Vigan appearance, lent by the shiny and ornate metal covers to the buggy, a style quite singular to this city.

Vigan is also known for crafts, particularly pottery, weaving and to some extent furniture making, and although these are very much tied to the city's long history, today production sites are largely in the modern part of the city. Pottery is particularly closely associated with Vigan, especially the production of large *burnay* jars used for pickling and general storage, the production of which can be seen at a couple of potteries on the westen edge of the city.

Coastal San Fernando

Above: Surf boards stacked up on San Juan beach, ready for action.

Right: Delicate lotus flowers add a softening, calming antidote to San Fernando's busy urban scene.

Far right: Using the small waves typical of the summer months, a very young girl makes surfing look all too easy.

Arguably containing the most accessible beaches north of Manila, the coastline north and south of the city of San Fernando includes long stretches of golden sand lapped by the waters of the South China Sea. To the south of the city is the coastal village of Bauang, San Fernando's first beach-resort area, developed originally as an American military rest and recuperation centre, and today – with the exception of a few resorts – fading as a beach attraction.

Most of the action now takes place at San Juan, a few kilometres north of the city. At the start of this century a small village that barely even made it onto the map, in a few short years San Juan has been transformed into a major surfing centre. The surfers are attracted by the wonderful waves that roll up to this shore almost every day from October to March, the height of the north-east monsoon.

SAN JUAN

When I first encountered San Juan in the late 1990s, while en route from Bauang to Vigan, my jaw dropped in amazement at the sight of this superb beach. It was caressed by some of the most perfect surfing waves I had ever witnessed in the Philippines, yet there was barely a single hotel to be seen. I could not believe that the place had yet to be discovered, despite being barely 100 m (330 ft) from the country's main north–south road.

Clearly someone with a more entrepreneurial spirit had the same thought at about the same time, for less than 15 years later the same place is now rated as one of the Philippines' premier surfing attractions. Much of today's development centres on the southern end of the beach, and there is plenty of accommodation to choose from. The much longer northern part, beyond Mona Liza Point, remains largely untouched, perhaps because the beach here shelves rather steeply.

During the main surfing months international competitions are a regular feature here. They are held mostly off Mona Liza Point, where the waves are at their biggest and best shaped. To the south the waves are generally much smaller, creating a great place for novices to learn the skills. Here, surfing instructors and board hirers are thick on the ground.

During the surfing off-months (generally April to September) the sea is mostly rather calm, making San Juan a beach for a bit of swimming and sunbathing. You will still see plenty of surfing novices having a go on the small waves; they are largely tiny children, the tousled-haired surfing dudes of tomorrow, making it look all too easy. The village of San Juan itself lies north of the beach, spread out along the north-south highway, and although it has no specific attractions it is a pleasant place to visit.

» TO THE CITY

When San Juan's beach and surf become too much, there is always San Fernando itself to explore, just a few kilometres to the south. It is a lively commercial centre and port, not unattractive and an absolute must for anyone who likes to watch street life – there is plenty of it here. For myself it centres on the market area, not so much within the enclosed, roofed section, but where it spills out onto the street under a series of colourful canopies and awnings. Here much of the produce is spread out on the ground, or on simple low stands. There is everything from cooking pans to herbal potions, honey, assorted fruits and vegetables, and – at the edges of the market – stalls selling satay chicken with coconut milk.

Away from the city centre to the west lies Poro Point, which was at one time an American military base and is now being developed as a freeport and tourism zone, complete with the glitzy Thunderbird Poro Point Hotel (built in a rather Mediterranean style, with a distinct 'Santorini' look to it), a vast golf course and a casino. On the other hand, 8 km (5 miles) to the east of the city, on nearby hills, is the complete antithesis, the wooded and very verdant Botanical Garden.

Above: A bright collection of beans and courgette flowers make for a single purchase item in the market.

Left: In San Fernando's colourful market, a shy trader takes refuge from the photographer behind a bowl, while a customer picks among her tomatoes.

» For cultural exploration, there is the Ma-Cho Temple. Although the Philippines is of course a largely Catholic country, the cities have a significant Chinese element, and San Fernando is no exception. Ma-Cho Temple is, for the visitor at least, the most visible manifestation of this, its colourful sweeping eaves and roofs climbing a hillside to the north of the city centre. Although this is essentially a Taoist temple largely dedicated to Matzu, the Goddess of the Sea (originally a historical figure from Fujian province, on the coast of south-east China) and protectress of fishermen, you will also see a number of Buddhist figures here, something that is quite typical of the rather eclectic religious style of Chinese temples almost everywhere.

Even for those who are not afficionados of Chinese temples, the uphill hike is still worthwhile. The temple grounds are a cool, peaceful oasis, draped in and shaded under dense foliage, with a rather thoughtful, contemplative atmosphere, and to top it all they provide a good viewpoint looking out across the city and port.

Right: Ma-Cho's pavilions and pagoda are a wonderful riot of colour and sculptured flying eaves, typical of Chinese temples all over Southeast Asia.

Far right: The dragon gate in front of the temple's main building frames a view across the city, bay and port.

Hundred Islands National Park

This glorious collection of islands nestles in a tight group in the sheltered waters of the Lingayen Gulf, off Luzon's north-west coast. Protected as a national park, these days run by the local government, Alaminos City, the 123 islands that make up the park are a popular weekend and holiday getaway, and one of the most lovely spots along Luzon's long coast.

ANCIENT CORAL REEFS

Covering an area of rather less than 20 square kilometres (8 square miles), the islands represent the eroded remains of a vast ancient coral reef left high and dry by falling sea levels at the end of the last ice age. Further sea erosion has undercut many of the islands, leaving them with curious mushroom shapes, which appear rather precarious.

Some of the islands are little more than jagged rocks protruding above the high-tide line, and many are impossible to land on due to their sheer, rocky cliffs.

However, a few have golden sandy beaches and are large enough to be worth exploring. Almost all are covered in dense scrubby vegetation, shrubs and trees that have adapted to be able to colonize and survive in the very thin, poor soil covering the coral limestone rocks.

It is all very picturesque and just the sort of place to visit by boat, exploring and island hopping in the calm, sheltered waters. Moreover, this ought to be a great place for snorkelling and diving, but unfortunately the islands and their surrounding waters and coral reefs have suffered from over-fishing and dynamiting down the years. This, coupled with cloudy water, has done untold damage to the marine environment. However, improved protection is believed to be slowly having a positive impact, allowing the recovery of corals, and an increase in the numbers of fish and even turtles to begin.

Above: Governor's Island's hilltop viewpoint gives a stunning panorama across many of Hundred Islands' forested limestone islands.

Left: A view looking downwards from steep rocks and through vegetation to the calm waters surrounding Governor's Island.

Far left: The islands are characterized by their sheer limestone sides, undercut by the action of the sea, surrounded by clear, rippling water and – in places at least – soft white sand.

» GETTING OUT TO THE ISLANDS

A boat is an absolute must for getting around Hundred Islands. You usually take a *banca*, the traditional Philippine outrigger boat, which can be hired at Lucap, a village on the edge of the city of Alaminos and the closest harbour to the islands.

There are a number of hotels and restaurants here and the national park has an office on the main jetty, where a nominal park-entrance fee is charged. It is also here that boat hire is organized, with fixed rates charged for trips to just the three main islands or for a wider exploration of the park.

Lucap's harbour can be a colourful and lively place. It serves not just the Hundred Islands' sightseeing boats but also the local fishermen, creating a busy and colourful scene of jostling boats. Unfortunately, the one downside is that expansion of the harbour to cope with the park's growing popularity has been done rather insensitively and carelessly. New wharves, roads and parking areas consist of little more than rubble dumped into the water with minimal effort to finish them off and tidy up their appearance. The result is a rather messy scene that the colour of the boats can only just distract attention away from.

Apart from that, once away from Lucap on your boat, you are transported into a world of blue and green. It is a 15-minute ride across open water to the first islands, and a chance, particularly if the wind is up, to get a good taste of salt spray, kicked up from the short, steep little waves by the *banca*'s outriggers – problematic if you are trying to hold a camera, wonderfully refreshing if you just want to cool off. Very soon, you're in calm waters, enveloped in a scene of islands ringed by jagged coralline rocks, topped by what appears to be just about impenetrable, densely tangled and verdant, almost irridescently green vegetation. The surrounding sea is the most perfect azure blue, a myriad of waterways splitting and rejoining as they wrap themselves around each shoreline, creating a host of complex channels, coves and bays, the perfect playground for people in boats.

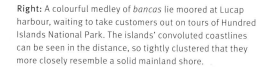

Right: A colourful medley of *bancas* lie moored at Lucap harbour, waiting to take customers out on tours of Hundred Islands National Park. The islands' convoluted coastlines can be seen in the distance, so tightly clustered that they more closely resemble a solid mainland shore.

» EXPLORING

Only three of the islands have any kind of development on them, in the form of beach facilities and huts, and these are Governor's, Children's and Quezon Islands. Not surprisingly, most visitors gravitate towards these islands, making them rather busy at weekends and during holidays. Quezon, near the northern limit of the island cluster, is arguably the busiest and most developed, with cafes and huts covering a large part of the island, and it also has the park's largest and best beach, not to mention great sunset views.

It is also possible to hire kayaks on Quezon Island. In these calm waters they provide a superbly peaceful way to explore many of the more remote islands, free from any crowd as well as the rattling noise of a *banca*'s engine, and allowing you to come in really close to some of the cliffs and other rock formations.

There are plenty of quieter islands to visit, places with such names as Marcos, Shell, Virgen, Cuenco and Sison's Islands, some with attractive small beaches and a few with caves to explore. An example of the latter is the seawater-filled Imelda Cave, on Marcos Island, where it is possible to dive into the water inside the cave, then swim through a low arch into the open sea and make your way back to a nearby beach.

Finally, birdwatching is increasingly popular in and around the Hundred Islands, with the mixed marine and woodland environment not surprisingly attracting a varied mix of bird types. Over 50 species have been identified in the area so far; there are Collared Kingfishers, terns, Philippine Ducks and Purple Herons in the marine environment, and Zebra Doves, monarchs, orioles and Blue-tailed Bee-eaters in the woodlands, to name just a few.

Right: The eerie blue waters and surrounding sheer walls of Imelda Cave, on Marcos Island. This is a popular place for swimmers as it is possible to swim from here, through a rock arch out into the sea and back to a nearby beach.

Baguio

The American colonial administration certainly knew what it was doing when in 1900, just one year after the US takeover of the Philippines, the city that is now Baguio was founded and developed as the country's summer capital. The comparatively short bus ride along the twisting, turning, climbing road from the coast to this city, 1,500 m (4,900 ft) up in the mountains, transports you not just to a new environment, but to a whole new climate zone. The stifling heat and humidity, along with the rice fields and coconut groves of the lowlands, give way to cool mountain air and the aromatic scent of pine trees. For visitors from countries with cooler climates, Baguio represents a welcome respite from the heat of the sea-level beach resorts, while lowland Filipinos may actually find it just a touch cold, particularly at night in December and January.

FROM THEN UNTIL NOW

When the Americans first arrived the site of Baguio was occupied by a small village called Kafagway, which was inhabited by Ibaloi people, one of the many distinct ethnic groups that to this day dwell in the mountain ranges of northern Luzon. By the time

Daniel Burnham (one of the USA's most famous architects and urban designers of the time) had finished, Kafagway had been replaced with a town laid out on a grid of streets, centred around Session Road, the main town-centre area, and nearby Burnham Park. Off to the east lay the colonial government areas and Camp John Hay, a vast military rest and rehabilitation centre.

Since then the city has been almost destroyed twice – during the Second World War, and more recently in 1990 by an earthquake – but the layout still remains much the same. Inevitably the city has grown vastly, however, and now sprawls over many of the surrounding hills. It is a confusing criss-crossing tangle of steep and twisting streets, many of them all too frequently clogged with engine-revving, smoke-belching traffic. The city long ago lost its national summer capital status, but it is still the commercial, industrial and administrative hub of the Cordillera, the mountain ranges that make up most of northern Luzon, capital of Benguet province and by far the largest city in the region.

Left: The tall spires of the city's relatively modern cathedral are a contrast to the historic Spanish churches more commonly seen in the Philippines.

Far left: A simulated miniature mountain scenery in the garden of the Manor, at the heart of Camp John Hay and one of Baguio's most exclusive hotels.

Above: At Mines View Park, a woman arranges traditional mountain tribe clothes on a stall that encourages visitors to dress up and be photographed.

» IN AND AROUND CAMP JOHN HAY

Camp John Hay and the old government areas remain a wonderful green oasis, together now mainly a civilian zone and significantly larger than the city-centre area. They are characterized by their dense stands of scented Benguet Pines – a species unique to the mountains of northern Luzon – and occasional views of the surrounding mountains, often barely glimpsed through the enveloping trees, along with deliberately winding roads and snaking woodland footpaths. Camp John Hay, though no longer a military site, is still a gated and controlled zone, which lends it a deliberate air of exclusivity. Its hilly roads, lawns and woodlands are carefully manicured, its rolling golf course (as well as the Baguio Country Club just outside the camp's gates) is populated largely by the Philippine elite, and its Manor is one the the most beautiful and prestigious hotels in the country.

To the north of the Camp there are various visitor attractions, including the Mansion, a colonial building that is still the official summer residence of the Philippine president, the rather small but attractive Botanical Garden and Mines View Park. The last of these is so named for the view it has across a huge valley containing an area of gold and copper mines, though these are in fact barely visible.

The real attraction, officially at least, is its wonderful early-morning view across the Cordillera Mountains, though you could be forgiven for thinking that the huge tangle of souvenir shops and stalls that all but block the path down to the main viewpoint is the real focus. Arguably the most entertaining of these offers visitors the chance to dress up in traditional tribal costumes and be photographed in front of the view.

Above: In the heart of leafy Camp John Hay stands The Mansion, the Philippine President's summer residence, though recent presidents have used it only rarely.

» **EXPLORING THE CITY**

One of the great attractions created by Baguio's cool climate is the huge array of temperate fruits and vegetables that can be grown in the region, produce that cannot be grown anywhere else in the Philippines. Foremost among these, in terms of fame at least, are strawberries, piles of which can be seen, along with much other produce both temperate and tropical, in the city-centre market. Best of all, however, is to head out to the suburbs to visit some of the city's many strawberry farms, at which it is possible to pick your own.

More traditional attractions include the Bell Church, an attractive Chinese Taoist temple, and Tam-Awan, a hillside re-creation of a village of the Ifugao people, the most prominent of the Cordillera's mountain ethnic groups, both in Baguio's northern suburbs. Not far away the Easter School of Weaving is a must-see place for anyone fond of woven products. Not only is there a well-stocked shop here, but it is also possible to spend as much time as you like watching the women working on traditional hand looms. Finally, right in the city centre, at the opposite end of Session Road from the market and close to Burnham Park's boating lake, stand the tall spires of the cathedral (see page 40), a rather modern building and quite distinct from the old Spanish architecture prevalent across most of the Philippines' churches.

Above: One of Baguio's most famous farm products is strawberries, due to the temperate climate prevalent at this altitude, and much sought after by Filipinos visiting from the lowlands.

Right and far right: One of the city's most visited attractions is the Bell Church, a lively hillside Taoist temple, whose bright colours, flying eaves and pagodas stand testament to the strength of the Chinese community.

Above: A local worker picks strawberries at one of the many strawberry farms around Baguio. Although it is popular for visitors to pick their own, often local staff will help them out, as here.

Sagada and the Halsema Highway

Baguio may well be the economic hub of the Cordillera, but for anyone really wanting to explore northern Luzon's mountains it is merely a pleasant gateway. To get immersed in the region you need to hit the Halsema Highway, heading northwards from its starting point in Baguio towards the town of Bontoc, a five-hour drive away, and almost certainly detouring just before Bontoc to visit the idyllic little mountain village of Sagada.

Driving along the Halsema Highway is no small undertaking. Until quite recently it was little more than a motorable dirt track regularly washed out by rain and landslides. Things have improved radically in the last few years – its entire stretch is now paved, making the journey a whole lot more comfortable and quicker. The road ducks and dives, twisting and turning through valleys and up and down mountains along its entire length, and offering spectacular views of pine-clad mountain ranges, first from one side of the vehicle, then from the other.

FOLLOWING THE HALSEMA

Along the way the road passes through villages and busy little market towns. In many areas the incredibly steep hillsides are cut into terraces, not for the rice fields more usually associated with a tropical country, but for the cultivation of the likes of potatoes, cabbages and tomatoes. The road climbs to a height of 2,255 m (about 7,400 ft), the highest point in the Philippine highway system, and although the signpost marking the spot may seem a little anti-climactic, the views more than make up for it, with a stupendous vista across a gaping valley eastwards towards Mt Pulag, at 2,930 m (9,610 ft) Luzon's highest mountain and the third highest mountain in the Philippines.

The road remains at high altitude for quite some time after this, though after crossing a mountain saddle, out of Benguet and into Mountain province, it starts to descend rapidly. The temperature climbs and the vegetation becomes ever more tropical, with potatoes and cabbages being replaced by rice and bananas. The road is now deep in a narrow valley, closely following the Chico River, the water rushing northwards towards its eventual union with the Cagayan River, the Philippines' longest waterway.

Finally, just before the town of Bontoc, you come to the turning off for Sagada, and once again you are on a road that climbs steeply and snakes endlessly up the mountainside. Terraced vegetable fields and dense pine forests begin to crowd around the road once again, and eventually it climbs into a high, hidden valley, where the first village houses start to appear. Initially there are just one or two here and there half-hidden among dense vegetation and limestone rock outcrops, but slowly they develop into a recognizable village. You have arrived.

Above: Along much of the route, the mountains are a patchwork of pine forest and vegetable fields terraced into the steep slopes.

Left: The Halsema Highway has some spectacular views of the surrounding Cordillera Central mountains, seen here at dawn just outside Baguio.

Right: The village of Sagada nestles picturesquely in a valley among pine woodlands and farmland.

Centre right: The region is typified by a patchwork of small terraced fields crammed with a range of temperate vegetables that include cabbages, potatoes, carrots, cauliflowers and much more.

Far right: Although high up in the mountains, many fields immediately around Sagada are able to cultivate rice.

» EXPLORING SAGADA

Sagada appeals to people in search of a peaceful rural retreat away from the rush and noise of the modern world. At an altitude of about 1,500 m (4,900 ft), it is wonderfully cool, particularly at night. This is really the place to relax in: to just sit back and take a deep breath, pulling in the fresh, pine-scented air. For just this reason, it has been attracting a steady trickle of travellers for many years, so Sagada is well equipped with inexpensive guesthouses and cafes, as well as an effective guiding system to help visitors find their way around this fascinating place.

Sagada is not just a mountain retreat, but also a place of great cultural interest. It is something of a centre for another of the mountain region's tribal peoples, the Applai, of which there are said to be about 178,000 scattered mainly around Mountain province. One of their most visible cultural traditions – which probably attracts the greatest visitor attention – is that of cave burial. Sagada is in an area of limestone riddled with caves, many of them containing coffins that have been piled up for hundreds of years. In a variation on this theme, coffins may be hung very visibly from cliffs, and there are a couple of examples of these close to the village.

Above: Sagadan weavers are renowned for their skill on hand-driven looms

Top right: Coffins attached to a cliff in Echo Valley, Sagada, the most visible manifestation of one of the Applai people's most traditional of customs, that of cave and cliff burial.

Right, below: A cloth on one of the looms illustrates the weavers' skill in creating the beautifully patterned textiles.

Far right, below: The entrance to Sumaguing Cave is a sloping chasm, littered with boulders and stalactites.

» Although it may seem natural to want to simply go walking around in Sagada's extraordinary countryside, it is likely that any such walking will become purposeful, aiming to visit at least a few of these cultural sites. Probably most accessible of all is Echo Valley, a small, densely wooded gorge just a few minutes' walk from the village centre, where a cluster of coffins can be seen at close quarters, attached to one of the cliffs. Such a collection of very publicly displayed coffins may seem a little incongruous to foreign eyes, but they do make for an oddly colourful and lively scene, representing something that is still central to Applai tradition, promoting the view that death is as much a part of life as life itself, is part of a 'journey', and is not something that should be hidden away. Beyond the coffins, the trail leads down into the densely wooded depths of the valley, leading eventually to Latang Cave, which can be walked through to the eastern edge of Sagada village on the opposite side. However, anyone wanting to do this really needs to have a guide, lighting and a readiness to get very wet.

Further away, at the southern end of the village, a short but steep hike along a path with stunning forest, mountain and valley views brings you to Lumiang Cave, where you will find over 100 coffins piled up, the oldest said to be over 500 years old, the newest dating from the 1980s. Still further on, lost in a deep, narrow gorge, you will come to the huge entrance to Sumaguing Cave. There are no burials here, but this cave is known for its stunning stalactites and stalagmites, not so much close to or in the entrance (though there are plenty here), but much deeper inside along a route that requires a guide and lights, as well as a willingness, once again, to get very wet.

When it comes to the culture of the living, the Sagadan Applai are also master craftsmen, particularly in pottery and weaving, and both can be watched at centres in or near the village. At Sagada Weaving, for example, not only is there a lovely shop but also it is possible to visit the workshop to watch the incredibly skilled weavers at work.

Without doubt Sagada's greatest asset, however, is that life here is so laid-back and peaceful that there is no pressure to rush around and visit any of these places. If all you want to do is sit on the guesthouse terrace with a cool drink, put your feet up and admire the misty, pine-clad hills, then that is just fine.

Banaue

On the eastern side of northern Luzon's Cordillera Mountain range sits what is arguably this region's most famous visitor attraction, the huge rice terraces that have been carved into the mountain slopes around the town of Banaue, collectively a UNESCO World Heritage Site.

Although Banaue town itself is not the prettiest of places, its location, down in a valley, clinging to steep hillsides and surrounded by lush, verdant mountains, is quite stunning. More significantly, it is the starting point for trips out to the surrounding villages where most of the rice terraces can be found, at settlements such as Batad, Hapao and Hungduan. Some terraces can also be seen at a series of viewpoints just a couple of kilometres north of Banaue, on the road towards Bontoc. However, these terraces are a mere shadow of what can be seen further afield, particularly at Batad, and are actually rather in decline.

The terraces were carved out of the sometimes almost sheer mountainsides about 2,000 years ago by the Ifugao people, one of the most prominent of the Cordillera's many tribal minorities, who still farm the terraces today. Quite apart from the incredible engineering feat that this would have represented so long ago, it is the extremely long period of continuous cultivation by generation after generation of the same ethnic group of people that has attracted global attention and led to the World Heritage Site accolade.

THE IFUGAO PEOPLE

This mountainous region is the cultural home of the Ifugao – indeed the entire province in which Banaue sits is named after them – and today they are believed to number almost 200,000. Throughout history they have been expert farmers, with rice as their main and in fact most prestigious crop. To this day they maintain many of their own traditions and customs, including a tendency to build their homes scattered across the rice fields, rather than in large and tightly packed communities. Apart from this most of their customs are mainly invisible to the casual visitor, though the oldest members of the society sometimes don their traditional clothes – brightly coloured jackets, skirts and/or loincloths, and hats – to pose for photographers at the main visitor spots around Banaue in return for a small fee.

The Ifugao also have a very distinct building style. Their houses consist of wooden posts and beams slotted together in joints, roofed with a pyramid-shaped thatch and without windows. The style is rapidly falling out of favour, alas, with at the very least thatch being replaced by sheet metal, if not the entire building style being done away with. Some traditional buildings can still be seen in the remoter villages, however, and there is an interesting museum of Ifugao building styles at Hapao.

Above left: A view along the hillside at Batad shows just how incredibly steep many of the rice terraces are, and just what an engineering feat it was to cut these from the mountain slopes.

Below left: At Hapao, a museum to Ifugao building styles preserves a collection of traditional buildings.

Far left: The village of Batad, high in the mountains above Banaue and at the heart of the most spectacular of the World Heritage rice terraces, is a centre of Ifugao tradition, where at least some of the buildings, as seen here, are still built in the historic wood and thatch style.

» EXPLORING THE TERRACES: HAPAO AND HUNGDUAN

The most accessible of the area's rice terraces are around the villages of Hapao and Hungduan, which are reachable by road in a couple of hours from Banaue. Neither of the villages is of great interest in itself, both consisting largely of diffuse collections of houses and farmsteads scattered across the sloping valley floor and up some of the steeper mountainsides, and strung out along the road that follows the valley.

The rice terraces are laid out mostly towards the valley floor. They are carved from relatively gentle slopes, creating a patchwork of carefully stepped emerald fields. Not surprisingly, the appearance of the fields varies greatly through the year, depending on the progress of the crop. The tiny seedlings are planted out from nurseries into the flooded fields at the end of the rainy season – usually in February or March – making the terraces resemble a myriad mirrors reflecting the sky, with just the occasional glimpse of blocks of irridescent green. Within a few months the plants have grown to fill the terraces, transforming them into a vast swathe of brilliantly vibrant emerald green, which in turn a few months later progresses to a russet or golden-yellow glow, shortly before harvest time.

Many of the terraces can be easily viewed from the road as it wends its way along the valley, but for the more energetic and adventurous it is easy enough to step off the road and simply follow the many paths that follow the terrace edges, criss-crossing the fields and passing by clusters of still moderately traditional Ifugao houses (with thatch roofs replaced by metal). It is the perfect way to breathe in some great fresh country air, and get up-close and personal with the vibrant green rice plants crowding in all around. Although most of the terraces are not that spectacular, one formation – called the Bacung spider web terraces – spreads across some of the steepest and most rugged of Hungduan's hillsides.

These pages: The slopes around Hungduan are significantly less steep than those at Batad, allowing much gentler terracing and hence larger fields. Furthermore, at this lower altitude you also see the occasional cluster of betel palms, which produce the betel nut that many mountain people chew endlessly, and which is responsible for the huge amount of damage done to their teeth and gums!

» **EXPLORING THE RICE TERRACES: BATAD**

By far the most spectacular terraces can be seen around the village of Batad, much higher up the mountains from Banaue, and reachable only on foot. Here you will find tier upon tier of terraces climbing the vertiginous slopes around an amphitheatre-like, bowl-shaped valley; from distant viewpoints the terraces resemble a vast array of theatre seats. Being at a higher altitude, the rice crop here runs about a month or so behind that seen at the much lower Hungduan. The latter's terraces are already a swathe of green at a time when Batad's farmers are still planting out their seedlings.

Houses cling to the hillside here and there, with another cluster down in the valley floor, surrounded by rice fields. There are a few simple guesthouses here – wonderful places to stay in overnight – so you do not need to visit simply on a day trip. It is reasonably straightforward to explore Batad's rice terraces, following the network of paths that criss-cross along the fields' walls. The steep slopes do make it rather strenuous, however, and be warned – with such steep terraces the narrow paths can be a dizzying height above the next field below.

There is also some great hiking to be done in the area, with footpaths radiating out from Batad to such places as Tappia Waterfall, less than an hour away, and towards other villages. Some routes make it possible to hike all the way back to Banaue.

Left: The village of Batad nestles among the rice terraces, clinging to one of the few less steep parts of the mountainside.

Far left: By far the most spectacular of Banaue's rice terraces are those around Batad, where fantastically narrow terraces have formed convoluted patterns as they follow the contours of the mountain face. Those few slopes that were too steep even for the Ifugao engineers/ farmers to terrace are still at least partially forested.

Manila

I have to admit that it is hard to describe Manila as one of the Philippines' most beautiful places. However, it is impossible to ignore the nation's capital, especially as it does have some very interesting aspects, though admittedly most are widely dispersed across the city.

Metro Manila, as the vast metropolis as a whole is officially described, is by far the Philippines' largest city, an aggregation of five cities, home to over 16 million people and growing every day. It is crowded, noisy and intense, but it is also fascinating, colourful and wildly alive. Although the gridlocked streets necessitate a calm, laissez-faire patience in getting around, it is worth digging out and exploring some of its gems.

HISTORICAL FEATURES

Most of the city's historical remains lie in and around Intramuros, the old Spanish walled settlement that sits at the mouth of Pasig River, at the heart of the official city of Manila itself. Fortunately its grid of narrow streets contains only light traffic, making Intramuros a very pleasant place to walk around in, particularly as all the points of interest are within relatively easy walking distance of each other.

Sadly, much of Intramuros's old architecture was destroyed during the Second World War, though the massively thick bastions and walls that surround it survived intact, along with Fort Santiago, which sits right on the river front and is itself an interesting place to explore. Another survivor is San Agustin Church, built at the end of the 16th century and the oldest church in the Philippines. How it has survived successive wars and earthquakes is anyone's guess, but survive it has, making it today arguably the country's greatest monument to the Catholic Church. The nearby Manila Cathedral has been less lucky – the present structure is the sixth cathedral on the site, with the present incarnation dating from 1958.

Left: A green oasis interspersed with ponds and fountains forms the centrepiece of Fort Santiago, the innermost bastion of Intramuros, the old walled town that was the capital of the Spanish Philippines.

Right and far right: Manila Cathedral, at the heart of Intramuros, is also very much at the heart of Philippine Catholicism. This relatively modern structure, built in 1958, replaced a much older cathedral destroyed by fighting near the end of the Second World War.

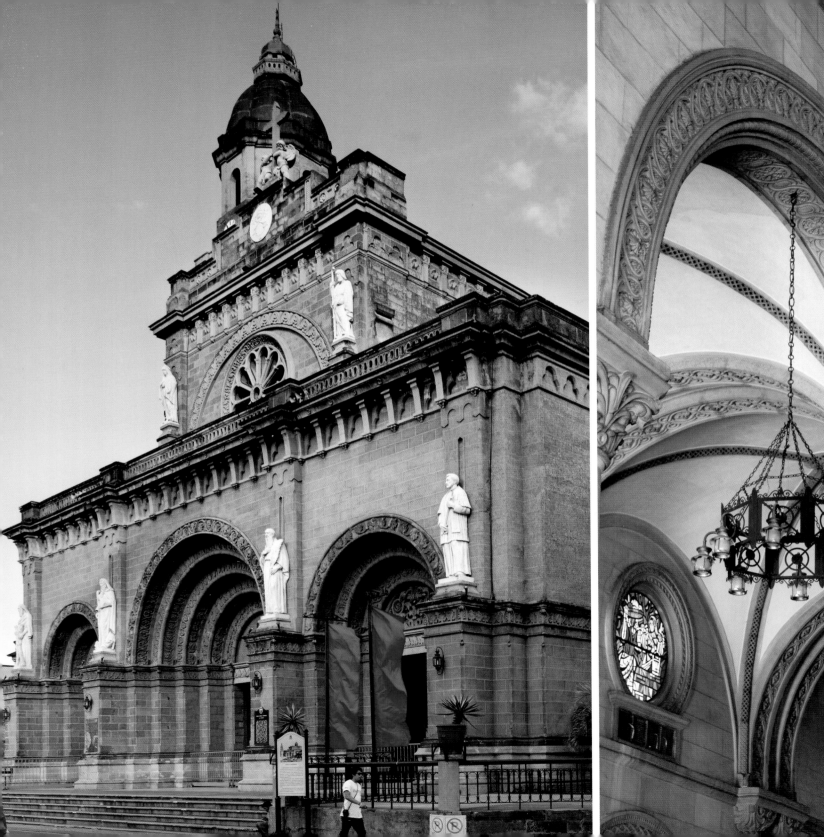

Right: Typical of the hotels along the bay, Traders Hotel has a top floor lounge with great evening views across the bay.

Far right: One of the features of the coastal part of Manila is the wonderful sunset views across Manila Bay, seen here from the roof of the Manila Hotel.

» Almost across the road from San Agustin Church is Casa Manila, a lovely re-creation of a colonial Spanish villa, with a great collection of antique furniture from the period, from harps and beds to dining tables and kitchen equipment. It is without doubt a beautiful showcase for the colonial era.

ACROSS THE RIVER

If you leave Intramuros behind and head northwards, crossing the Pasig River, you arrive in a wholly different environment. Here you find yourself in the Manila districts of Binondo and Quiapo, some of the most crowded areas in Southeast Asia. Historically Spanish Manila's Chinese settlement, this was for many years the hub of Manila's business community. To this day the narrow streets are still packed with small businesses, and a crowded market keeps the place filled with a buzzing energy. This is very much the place for people watching, as well as for looking out for a wealth of Philippine natural products from bananas and herbal remedies, to fresh and dried fish.

The eastern fringe of this market sits at Plaza Miranda, on the northern side of which stands Quiapo Church, home to one of the Philippines' most important religious icons. This is the statue of the Black Nazarene, a carving of Jesus made from ebony in Mexico in the 18th century, then brought here. On 9 January every year the statue is paraded through these streets in front of huge, jostling crowds.

FROM RIZAL PARK TO THE MALL OF ASIA

Heading south from Intramuros, and after negotiating a tangle of main roads, you come to Rizal Park, a vast, open green space commonly known as Luneta. Site of the 1898 execution of José Rizal, national hero and father of an independent Philippines, this is a rare piece of parkland in an otherwise crowded city. Its fountains and shady groves attract hordes of Manileños, particularly on Sundays. The park contains an open-air theatre that has occasional cultural performances, which are frequently free on Sundays. To the east stands the National Museum of the Filipino People, a huge exhibition of the country's history and culture. Across the street is the newly renovated National Gallery of Art.

From the park you can continue southwards along the bayside promenade which parallels the main traffic artery that is Roxas Boulevard. Palm tree-lined and remarkably serene despite the nearby traffic, the promenade is a wonderful place to watch the sunset over Manila Bay (complete with silhouettes of anchored ships) and the distant mountains of the Bataan Peninsula.

Above: At street level, a promenade follows Roxas Boulevard, providing a popular spot to relax and watch the sun go down at the end of a working day.

Right: A view of affluence, in this image taken across Manila Marina towards some of the new and rapidly growing tower blocks in the Malate district.

Centre right: Rather less affluent, but more lively and colourful is the crowded market in Quiapo and Binondo.

Far right: At the far southern end of Manila's coast, the brand new Mall of Asia, a hugely popular shopping centre, is decorated with some abstract modern architecture.

» The promenade takes you down as far as the Manila Yacht Club, the marina and the nearby Cultural Center of the Philippines, and from here it is best to take a taxi across to the next and newest stretch of seafront, the Mall of Asia. A vast new bay-side shopping complex, this is almost a small town in itself, and a pleasant one at that. Quite apart from its shopping 'streets' and terraces, it is fronted by an attractive shore-side promenade complete with snack stalls and a ferris wheel, which gets packed with strolling, relaxing Manileños every evening.

MAKATI AND MANDALUYONG
Moving eastwards and inland you come to the main business hubs of modern Metro Manila, the twin cities of Makati and Mandaluyong. The modern face of business-savvy Manila, both have towering skylines of concrete and glass. Makati in particular is filled with offices, glitzy hotels and upmarket shopping malls. It is all a very far cry from the rather down-at-heel scenes of Binondo and some other districts of old Manila, but they all come together to make a complete picture of this pulsating city.

Taal Lake and Volcano

In a landscape littered with volcanoes, Taal manages to be one of the most famous and most visited. At first glance one might be forgiven for wondering why. After all, it is rather small and appears to be quite innocuous. It is, however, extraordinarily beautiful. The volcano is set on an island in a lake, which is within a huge volcanic crater, lying in the southern part of Luzon, itself of course an island. Moreover, it is one of the Philippines' most active and most dangerous volcanoes, with 33 eruptions since records began in 1572 and its latest eruption occurring in 1977. This last fact alone makes another eruption well overdue, something that has the Philippine Institue of Volcanology and Seismology (PHIVOLCS) constantly monitoring the volcano.

That fact ought also to put anyone well and truly off visiting the place, but human nature being what it is, the possible danger simply acts as an extra attraction. Visitors are keen to experience a little of the 'living on the edge', and to see what a sleeping but nevertheless smouldering giant actually looks like. Conveniently, Taal is also very accessible, just 60 km (37 miles) south of Manila, with good roads right to the lake's shore and plenty of boat-riding opportunities out to Volcano Island, ground zero for all the activity.

Left: A view across the incredible Taal volcano, clearly showing the lake filling the main crater, with the vast expanse of Taal Lake beyond, surrounding Volcano Island on which this volcano sits.

ABOUT TAAL

The whole volcano-and-lake complex is contained within the vast Taal caldera, the remains of an enormous volcano that must originally have stood about 5,500 m (18,000 ft) high, but which exploded and collapsed at some point in the geological past. Today the caldera as a whole is about 30 km (20 miles) across and its walls are less than 700 m (2,300 ft) high. From its rim there are great views across Taal Lake and the volcano.

Today's caldera lake used to be a coastal bay linked to the sea to the south, but a series of eruptions in the 18th century sealed it off, and since then it has gradually lost its salinity until today it is a completely freshwater lake. Quite a number of marine fish got a bit of a surprise when they found they could no longer venture out to sea, and in the intervening years several have evolved into new freshwater species. The most well known of these are the Freshwater Sardinella (the world's only freshwater sardine, known locally as *tawalis*) and the venomous Garman's Sea Snake, both of which are unique to Taal Lake. Several other such unique species have been wiped out by human pressure, including Bull Sharks, and both the Freshwater Sardinella and the Garman's Sea Snake are now under pressure.

» Volcano Island, sitting in the middle of the caldera lake, is itself only about 5 km (3 miles) long, yet it is covered with no fewer than 47 cones and craters. The largest is the main crater, the floor of which contains another lake, the epicentre for nearly all of the island's eruptions since 1572, though not the most recent series. Its last eruption was in 1911, at which time the crater lake was formed. The majority of eruptions since then, including the most recent one, in 1977, have come from the nearby but much smaller Mt Tabaro. Intriguingly, with a maximum height of 311 m (1,023 ft), Taal is the world's smallest active volcano, belying the magnitude of its potential threat.

EXPLORING TAAL

Most visits to the Taal Volcano begin with the views from Tagaytay, a town sitting in the cool air on top of the caldera rim. From here the entire lake is visible, along with Volcano Island, though the island's main crater is difficult to make out. Instead, the most prominent feature is a cinder cone, Binintiang Malaki, which towers above the island's shore and is the nearest point on the island to Tagaytay. As a result it generally fools first-time visitors into believing that it is the main crater, rather than the far less visible smudge half hidden behind it.

To get out to Volcano Island you need to head down to the lakeside town of Talisay, where it is easy to hire a *banca* for the 20-minute ride across the lake. When you arrive at the island you are greeted by plenty of would-be guides – though they are not really needed – as well as offers of pony rides to the volcano's crater. While the lake crossing is cool and refreshing, the hike from the island's shore to the crater rim along what is known as the Spanish Trail is hot and sweaty – unless of course you decide to take one of those ponies. The trail is not difficult – just a rather steady 45-minute climb – but the surrounding vegetation is rather short and offers no shade at all.

Above: The lovely soft pastel colours of a bougainvillea bush decorate the garden of a hotel in the village of Talisay, on the shores of Lake Taal, one of the best bases for exploring Volcano Island.

Left: Although Volcano Island is officially an exclusion zone with no one allowed to live on it, many families do, eking a living by acting as guides and by fishing in the lake, as testified by the line of *bancas* permanently moored along the island's shore.

Below: A view across Taal Lake from the upper slopes of the volcano, looking across to the distant shore that is the wall of the huge Taal caldera surrounding both the lake and Volcano Island.

» Once at the crater rim you are treated to a
spectacular view across a surprisingly vast abyss
(how could this possibly be almost invisible from
Tagaytay?), at the bottom of which are the green,
shimmering waters of the crater lake, complete with
a few smouldering fumaroles along its shore, and
yet another little island (called Vulcan Point) in the
middle of the lake. Beyond, Taal Lake can be seen
surrounding the island volcano, itself hemmed in
by the outer caldera walls, and beyond this can be
glimpsed the sea.

From the crater rim further exploring possibilities are
rather limited, though other trails can be followed
elsewhere on the island, including a hike leading to
the summit of Mt Tabaro. There is also a path down
to the shore of the crater lake, though this is usually
off-limits whenever volcanic activity increases.

Above: A view from the lake shore at Talisay to Binitiang
Malaki, a large cinder cone and one of Volcano Island's
highest peaks, though not currently an active crater.

Right: A peaceful dusk view from Talisay across Taal Lake
to Volcano Island, silhouetted against the distant light.
Binitiang Malaki is the large cone on the far right.

Mindoro & Palawan

Largely rural regions, these two provinces are often thought of as the Philippines' wild frontier.

Mindoro is a very mountainous island with some of the country's highest peaks, providing a major, rewarding challenge for the serious and experienced hiker. In general, however, road links are difficult and getting around can be rather slow. As a result, only a few places in Mindoro attract visitors in any great numbers, and top of this short list is Puerto Galera, a lovely peninsula lined with beaches and coral reefs almost at the island's northern tip.

Palawan, on the other hand, is without doubt the Philippines' capital for ecotourism; its relatively low population density and reasonably effective conservation measures ensuring that the region is rich in unspoiled wild areas. It is home to some of the most beautiful places in the whole of Southeast Asia, mostly along the coast and incorporating stunning beaches, islands and coral reefs, the best known of which include Honda Bay, El Nido and Puerto Princesa Subterranean River.

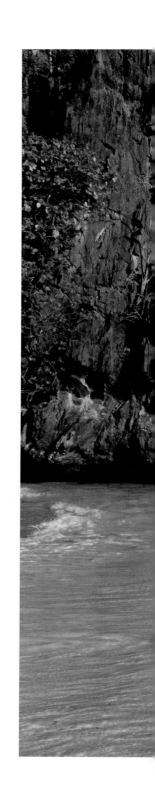

A *banca* brings visitors up to Seven Commandos Beach, in Palawan's El Nido, a beautiful location in one of the most stunning corners of the Philippines.

Puerto Galera

Puerto Galera is one of the Philippines' most popular visitor attractions, and with good reason. Sitting close to the northern tip of Mindoro, it is an absolute jewel, consisting of a wonderfully verdant peninsula coupled with a group of islands that together create a fabulous natural harbour, Muelle Bay, at the innermost end of which sits Puerto Galera town. Strung out along both the peninsula and the coast west of the town is a collection of beaches (no less than 32 according to the literature), while offshore and beneath the waves are some of the Philippines' most well-protected coral reefs.

Diving is big here, particularly for the resorts clustered around the peninsula's beaches, as these are the closest to the marine reserve, protecting the best reefs. Beach worshippers with less inclination to dive head to the western beaches, which certainly have by far the best of Puerto Galera's sand.

Behind the beaches the land quickly rises into a series of mountains. The highest is Mt Malasimbo (1,228 m/4,028 ft), which is partially forested and criss-crossed with a number of good hiking trails (at least on the lower slopes), and is the preserve of the Mangyan, Mindoro's indigenous people.

So important from the conservation perspective is the combined environment of onshore mountain forest and offshore submarine coral reef that in 1973 UNESCO declared the entire Puerto Galera area, from the reefs to the mountaintops, a 'Man and the Biosphere Reserve', part of a global network of vitally important natural sites. In the 40 or so years since then, protection of the reefs has worked well through a combined local effort, while population and commercial pressures have been less kind to the mountains, though to this day patchy forest survives, particularly on the upper slopes.

With no airport and no road access from anywhere outside of Mindoro, and with the great majority of ferries running from Batangas consisting simply of very large bancas, a trip to Puerto Galera still feels like something of an adventure, particularly for anyone coming directly from Manila and with little experience of rural Philippines. And yet, Puerto Galera is by far the most accessible part of Mindoro, large areas of this rugged island being extremely remote. As such, Puerto Galera is a good starting point for adventures further into Mindoro, at least for those with plenty of time and a tolerance for the island's rough, slow roads.

Above: A group of scuba divers prepares to head out from Puerto Galera's Big La Laguna Beach.

Right: Colourful soft corals adorn the walls of the Puerto Galera reefs.

Mindoro & Palawan

» MUELLE BAY AND THE TOWN

The starting point for almost anyone coming to Puerto Galera is the lovely Muelle Bay natural harbour and Puerto Galera town itself. Barely 130 km (80 miles) south of Manila, the vast majority of people arriving here come by ferry from the port of Batangas on the mainland, itself only a couple of hours' drive from the capital.

As the ferry approaches the densely green peninsula it is hard to understand where it is going. Soon enough, however, a narrow passage opens up, leading into an almost completely enclosed bay, the perfect natural harbour, surrounded by sandy beaches and vibrantly green coconut groves. Muelle Bay has been a valuable protected anchorage for many hundreds of years. The Spanish arrived in 1572 and came to use it as a place for repairing their galleons; they gave it today's name – Puerto Galera, or Port of Galleons. Present-day yachts use the same anchorage, in continuation of an ancient tradition.

Journey's end comes at Puerto Galera's wharf, a harbourside wall lined with cafes and souvenir stalls, the town itself largely hidden from view among the trees. Although it is a pleasant place few people linger here, most moving quickly over to a *banca* or jeepney to take them on the relatively short ride to one of the beaches.

THE WESTERN BEACHES

Three main beaches are lined up along the coast west of Puerto Galera town, the largest and most easterly being White Beach. This really is a quite stunning beach, a long and wide, dazzlingly white stretch of coral sand. It is also the most developed and busiest of all the beaches, with plenty of hotels and resorts, attracting thousands of visitors during peak times.

Further west, and more remote, smaller and quieter are Aninuan and Talipanan Beaches, both of which are definitely rather more upmarket. For those who want to explore the mountains, these are good places to be based in, with the closest access. The hike from Talipanan to Talipanan Falls, for example, takes less than an hour each way.

Right: A fishing village nestles among coconut palms on the sheltered shore of lovely Muelle Bay, one of the central features of Puerto Galera.

» THE PENINSULA'S BEACHES

These consist principally of Sabang, Small La Laguna and Big La Laguna Beaches, which are strung out along the outermost reaches of the peninsula from east to west, and reached from the town most easily by *banca*. The main attraction of all three is diving, which is just as well because it has to be admitted that the sand is not great at any of them – in many places it is rather patchy and pebbly, if not totally rocky. Add to that the huge numbers of *bancas* lined up along the shore and there really is not a whole lot of space left for the sunbathers.

DIVING

Long-term work to protect the reefs off this peninsula has in general done a good job, due largely to the clear connection between the state of the reefs and the state of the local economy. Coupled with the hugely varied environment – quiet, sheltered coves and sandy bays, versus exposed and rocky cliffs and drop-offs – the result has been to provide a fantastic diving experience, with dive sites that vary from shallow and easy, safe for snorkellers and novice divers, to deep and rough, suitable only for the most experienced. In the case of some dive sites, just their names give good clues to suitability: Coral Garden tends to indicate a calm, gentle kind of place, whereas Shark Cave and the Washing Machine are not likely to instil confidence in a novice, and with good reason.

With so many long-established and well-run dive operators working out of the peninsula's beaches, and with such a huge diversity of dive sites to choose from, Puerto Galera is not surprisingly one of the best places in the Philippines both for first-timers to come to learn to dive, and for experienced divers to get a taste of some of the best diving in Southeast Asia.

Above: A *banca*, moored at Small La Laguna beach, nuzzles its bow right up to the very edge of the water, illustrating just how shallow a draught these boats have.

Left: Small La Laguna beach, seen here in very early morning sunlight, is slightly more spacious. than nearby Big La Laguna.

Far left: Despite its name Big La Laguna beach can get rather crowded, with the shore lined with lodges jostling for position.

Puerto Princesa Subterranean River National Park

Lying about 80 km (50 miles) north of Puerto Princesa, the provincial capital, this is almost certainly Palawan's number one attraction.

A 22,000 ha (54,000 acre) national park (until a few years ago known as St Paul's Underground River National Park) on Palawan's north-west coast, it has a rugged, mountainous karst limestone landscape that is largely forested and falls away steeply to golden sand beaches and mangrove swamps along the coast.

It is hugely important from a biodiversity perspective, but the main attraction for visitors is the underground river that flows for 8.2 km (5 miles) through the limestone mountains before flowing out onto a beach and into the sea. Frequent tours in boats that are little more than tiny dugout outrigger canoes take visitors from the forested shore of a lagoon at the cave's mouth on torchlit tours for just over 1km upriver into the total darkness of the cave, before returning to the dazzlingly bright daylight and the lagoon.

From the environmental perspective, the underground river – though hugely interesting and of importance geologically – is secondary to the national park's wildlife conservation role. Ironically, few visitors pay much attention to this, heading straight to the lagoon and the tours of the underground river, giving wildlife only cursory attention in terms of the few species that can be seen around this small area. However, the Puerto Princesa Subterranean River National Park is, in fact, a globally important refuge for Southeast Asian wildlife, a fact readily appreciated by those who do explore either the mountainous inland forest trails or the extensive riverine mangroves.

GLOBAL RECOGNITION

It is clear that the world's major conservation organizations have come to appreciate the park's importance, for since its formation in 1971 it has been showered with accolades, starting in the 1970s with its designation by UNESCO as a 'Man and the Biosphere Reserve', and followed in the 1990s by its award as a World Heritage Site. This, in turn, was followed by its classification as a Ramsar Site (a wetland of global wildlife importance), an Important Bird Area and a National Geological Site. In late 2011 it was voted by an international panel to be one of the world's New Seven Wonders of Nature (along with such places as Amazonia, Halong Bay in Vietnam and Komodo Island in Indonesia).

Above: From the cave, the river enters a lagoon, then flows through a channel, across the beach and into the sea.

Right: Exploring just a small part of the huge underground river is by far the main visitor attraction.

» THE PARK'S LANDSCAPE

The park's rugged landscape is dominated by the dome-shaped mountain, the 1,028 m (3,372 ft) high Mt St Paul's, so named in 1850 (according to the story) by British sailors passing by, who found that the mountain reminded them of London's St Paul's Cathedral.

Much of the underlying rock is karst limestone, which being extremely porous and easily eroded is riddled with caves. The biggest of these is believed to be 22 km (13 miles) long, with the northernmost 8.2 km (5 miles) of it occupied by the Cabayagan River. The cave has recently been found to contain at least two levels, resulting in several waterfalls within the cave system. Until quite recently this was believed to be the world's longest underground river, but a much longer one has been discovered in the Yucatan of Mexico.

The last 4 km (2½ miles) of the underground river are tidal, making the water increasingly salty as the river nears the cave's mouth. Here the water flows out of a comparatively low, barely visible entrance overhung with stalactites; it then enters a lagoon surrounded by rainforest and separated from the sea by a sandbar. A narrow channel carries the water across the beach to the sea, though much of the lagoon also simply drains through the sand and into the sea that way.

BIODIVERSITY

The park still consists of a complete sea-to-mountaintop ecosystem (increasingly rare today), ranging from shoreline forests (mangroves and beach forest), through lowland and limestone rainforests, up to montane rainforest on the mountain's upper slopes. In all, the park contains eight of the 13 tropical rainforest types known to exist in Asia, with over 800 species of plant – one-third of all the plant species so far identified in Palawan – 295 of them trees.

In terms of animal wildlife, 254 vertebrate species have been identified in the park, the most easily observed of which are the Long-tailed Macaques and monitor lizards frequently seen in the forest around the park-ranger station. Birds make up the great majority of species, and include all 15 that are endemic, or unique, to Palawan, including the Tabon Scrubfowl (a chicken-like bird that can sometimes be seen in the forest around the ranger station), the Palawan Peacock-pheasant and the Palawan Hornbill. Offshore, in the marine part of the park, the coral reef is largely in good condition. Several species of turtle can be seen there, while seagrass beds in shallow, sandy-bottomed waters are home to the highly threatened Dugong, a very calm but shy marine mammal that sadly is rarely seen.

Top: Monitor lizards, many up to 2 metres (6½ feet) long, often hang around the ranger station, looking for leftover food. Though they appear ferocious, they are usually quite approachable.

Above: The Crab-eating, or Long-tailed Macaque is easily seen around the lagoon and in the forest close to the boat landing area.

Left: Close to the shore the forest changes to include plants that can flourish in salty conditions, such as these pandanus plants.

Far left and below: Much of the forest grows on very poor, thin soil overlying highly porous, coralline limestone, making growth conditions difficult. As a result, much of the forest consists of a dense tangle of small trees, interspersed with occasional giants that are often held up with buttress roots.

» VISITING THE PARK

All the park's accolades have resulted in rapidly growing numbers of visitors, all of them wanting to go to just the one spot – the entrance to the underground river – putting growing pressure on both local infrastructure and the park's conservation role. As a result of this, visitor numbers have now been capped by the Puerto Princesa city government, which runs the park, and anyone wanting to make the trip has to book in advance, often quite some time ahead.

For those with a reservation it is easy enough to reach the park. The road from Puerto Princesa is now paved all the way (after years of being a very bumpy track alternating between dust and deep mud, depending on the time of year), and frequent tours are available from the city's hotels. The road leads to the village and harbour of Sabang, a few kilometres west of the national park – itself a site of a magnificent beach and several resorts – from where *bancas* can be hired for the 15-minute ride to the park. Alternatively, it is possible to hike up the coast from Sabang along a 5 km (3 mile) forest trail that takes from one to two hours to complete.

If you go by *banca*, then once in the park you will be dropped off at a beach, from where it is a five-minute walk through forest to a lagoon and the starting point for boat tours of the underground river. Here you register, take a life-jacket and helmet, and await your turn. There is usually quite a crowd of people here, so it will not be the peaceful wild experience that you might hope for.

Left: From the outside, the river's exit from the cave and into the lagoon is barely visible, virtually hidden by overhanging rocks, stalactites and dangling vines.

Far left: Inside the subterranean river the calm water reflects the sheer rock walls of the tunnel, a scene that has been unchanged for millennia.

Right: Beautiful Sabang beach, just outside the southern edge of the national park, and starting point for boat rides up to the underground river.

Right: A view of the dense and tangled mangroves that line both sides of the Sabang River, creating an intensely primeval scene and a sense of a still wild nature.

Inset: A deadly Mangrove Snake lies curled up in a mangrove tree above the water.

» The boats are small outrigger canoes that will hold up to 12 people plus the boatman, who quietly paddles you across the calm waters while giving a commentary. Whoever gets the front seat has the job of holding a floodlight to illuminate the otherwise total darkness inside the cave. Lasting about an hour, and heading upriver just over a kilometre into the cave, the tour passes a number of huge stalactite and stalagmite formations, the cave's height varying from just a few metres to huge chambers. Throughout the tour swiftlets and bats flit and swoop past the boat, providing a twittering background soundtrack.

Apart from taking the underground river tour, you can explore the forest via a couple of marked jungle trails, one of which is the path back to Sabang. For the best chance to see macaques and monitor lizards, all you have to do is to hang around the park-ranger station close to the boat dock.

On the edge of the park, between the park itself and Sabang, you can explore an extensive mangrove swamp along the Poyuy-Poyuy River. Guides from a local community business take you in paddled outrigger canoes deep into this primeval, tangled forest. Macaques are commonly seen in the forest along the way, and it is likely that your guide will be able to pick out the occasional snake curled up in the trees. This is wild Palawan at its best, with the natural forest all around, and the shrill call of cicadas and the sound of the boat's paddle gently dipping into the water the only sounds. It makes you feel as though you have stepped into a Joseph Conrad novel.

Above: The mouth of the Sabang River, where it emerges from dense mangroves then flows out across sandflats and into the sea. A beautiful tropical scene.

Honda Bay

Right: A tiny rivulet of sparkling water cuts a curved path across Cowrie Island's white sand and into the azure sea, with the hills of mainland Palawan in the distance.

Far right: Cowrie Island is arguably the most popular.

Right on the outskirts of Palawan's provincial capital, Puerto Princesa, Honda Bay is among the loveliest of the Philippines' many bays of spectacular coral islands ringed with blindingly white sand and azure sea. This is the quintessential tropical coral heaven, a scattering of very low-lying sandy islands set in a calm, very shallow, very clear sea, with coconut palms, sandbars, stunning blues and beautiful submarine corals all part of an average day.

That said, the bay and its islands are very accessible from Puerto Princesa, so they can get quite busy, especially at the weekends and during holidays. At these times anyone wanting to play at Robinson Crusoe might be a little disappointed, particularly if they head out to any of the main islands.

ABOUT THE ISLANDS

Honda Bay's 16 islands are all remnants of ancient coral reefs left behind when sea levels fell, set in a vast bed of soft white sand on a very shallow shelf close to the mainland shore. All the islands are flat and very low lying. They are partially covered with rather scrubby vegetation, and have sandy beaches along parts of the shores and mangroves elsewhere. Vast sandbars exposed only at low tide cover areas larger than the islands that they are linked to.

» Corals provide good snorkelling below the low tide line close to some of the islands, and also attract several endangered species of turtle. Sandy areas covered with beds of seagrass provide a home to the rare Dugong. Due to the shallowness of the waters, the shoals of pelagic fish typical of areas with deeper water, such as trevally and barracuda, are just not seen here, but it is usual to see large numbers of small and very colourful reef fish.

Fishermen work the bay extensively, and fishing villages line both the mainland shore and a couple of the islands. As a consequence – especially as the local population is growing all the time – fish stocks in the bay are under pressure. It is very common to find fish traps set up among the mangroves, always a favourite hiding place for a good many marine species.

LOOKING AROUND THE ISLANDS

Any trip out into Honda Bay starts at Santa Lourdes, a small village a few kilometres north of Puerto Princesa. It is a pretty little place with many of its houses barely visible, so well are they hidden among a mass of coconut palms, acacia trees and various shrubs, with an assortment of boats under repair or construction right among the houses. Most of the houses are strung out along a road that leads to the Santa Lourdes wharf, where *bancas* line up ready to take anyone out on a tour of the islands.

The most visited of the islands are Cowrie, Pandan, Starfish and Snake Islands. The first of these is named after the huge number of cowrie shells found on its beach, Pandan Island for the pandanus trees that line its shore, Starfish Island (not surprisingly) for the many starfish found here, and Snake Island not for snakes, but for the fact that its long, narrow and curving sandbar keeps changing shape with the rising and falling tides. One final place is Lu-li islet, actually short for '*lulubog-lilitaw*', meaning that the island goes up and down – actually it is just a sandbar that appears only at low tide and is completely submerged at high water.

Left: The coconut palms behind Cowrie Island's beach provide both shade and space for picnicking. However, the perennial danger of falling coconuts makes it unwise to stay for too long right at the base of a tree!

Mindoro & Palawan

» Most of the islands have at least one spectacular beach, lapped by calm, crystal-clear waters, ideal for cooling off, a gentle swim or generally just lazing around. Almost all are within easy reach of good snorkelling areas with healthy corals and colourful reef fish. Cowrie island has a cafe, blessed with the freshest and most refreshing coconuts, straight from the surrounding palms. Anyone going for a walk beyond the beach on almost any island will probably find themselves in extensive mangroves, which can be great to explore at low tide. On Pandan Island, for example, it is possible to walk for several kilometres across a vast sandflat, skirting the seaward edge of a mangrove swamp. You are absolutely high and dry, with the sea at this state of the tide hundreds of metres away. This is the best and easiest time to explore the mangroves; a good time to spot fiddler crabs hiding among the trees' aerial routes, or to catch the flashing irridescent blue of a Collared Kingfisher as it charges from tree to tree. Flowerpeckers, tiny but very colourful little birds, are also often seen in these mangroves, along with birds more typical of the shoreline such as Reef Egrets and Little Herons.

The furthest flung of the islands is 20 ha (49 acre) Arreciffe, which is owned and occupied by the luxury Dos Palmas Island Resort and is the only accommodation on this little archipelago. Come here to really get away from it all in a stunning location, without, of course, leaving behind life's little luxuries.

Above: Often reasonably tolerant of human presence, the Pacific Reef Egret is frequently seen on Palawan's beaches, particularly when – as with this bird – they are engrossed in hunting for dinner.

Right: A small fishing *banca* lies drawn up under trees and at the high tide line on Pandan Island's main beach.

El Nido and the Bacuit Archipelago

It is so easy to become a little glib about all the superlatives that it is tempting to throw around to describe some of the Philippines' landscapes and seascapes, particularly in Palawan, yet every single one is fully justified when it comes to the El Nido area. It is difficult to understate its incredible beauty, for I cannot help feeling that it is one of the most stunning places I have ever seen in the tropical world.

It has to be admitted that the commercial centre, namely El Nido town itself, is growing and starting to become a touch chaotic, but its setting on the shore of a sweeping natural harbour, hemmed in by high, sheer limestone cliffs and mountains, is second to none. Couple that with the view out to offshore islands, similarly ringed with sheer limestone cliffs, forming the gateway to Bacuit Bay and its scattering of limestone islands, rocks and beaches, and you have the feeling that you are in some kind of paradise.

RUGGED CLIFFS AND SANDY BEACHES

El Nido town, the centre for communications and much of the area's accommodation, shops and restaurants, sits in its own small bay, ringed by spectacular cliffs, at the northern end of the island-studded Bacuit Bay.

Despite what I have already said about the place, El Nido town is not unpleasant, with a friendly, relaxed atmosphere. It is laid out along a beach that is lined with cafes and lodges, with a wharf and *banca*-crammed harbour at its western end, close against towering limestone cliffs. From the beach there is a view westwards to the hulking outline of Cadlao Island, the largest of Bacuit's islands and with its highest point, at 640 m (2,099 ft), creating a powerful, rugged silhouette at sunset. It is a view to quietly contemplate as the evening light fades to night, a beer in hand, the soft sand beneath your feet.

Right: The bay that forms El Nido town's harbour is in one of the most beautiful settings imaginable, set against a stunning backdrop of rocky islands.

Centre right: The harbour, and indeed much of the town too, is hemmed in by a line of high limestone cliffs, further adding to the splendour of the setting.

Far right: Although El Nido town is growing and getting busier, it is still a pleasant, green place with a slow pace of life.

» Guarding Bacuit Bay's northern entrance, Cadlao is just the taster for what lies beyond. To the south the islands stretch away into the distance, 45 of them according to official figures; almost all are big, solid blocks of limestone, ringed with sheer, jagged cliffs. These are not the low-lying pancakes of Honda Bay, but rugged, mountainous hunks of rock thrusting up from the bay floor and towering above the sea's surface. Many have just about no landing places, but others have spectacular white-sand beaches. There are somewhere between 50 and 100 beaches, depending on who you believe; not one of them is accessible by road and all require a boat.

Most of the less rugged islands, along with much of the adjoining mainland, are cloaked in dense rainforest ranging from mangroves and beach forest along the marine shores, through lowland evergreen rainforest inland, to limestone forest with trees specialized to survive on the poor, thin soil covering the steep and highly porous rocks. They are all a valuable refuge for Palawan's animal wildlife, including all of its endemic birds, such as the Palawan Hornbill and Palawan Scops Owl, as well as other endangered birds that are not restricted to Palawan, like the Philippine Cockatoo.

Above: This sheer limestone cliff on Lagen Island is typical of the ruggedness of the Bacuit islands.

Left: A sunset view from near El Nido town of Cadlao Island, the largest and highest of the Bacuit archipelago.

95

» Beneath the bay's calm waters the coral reefs did suffer some damage due to dynamite fishing in years gone by, but today they are recovering. Many of the beaches, as well as several lagoons created by inlets in the cliffs, have excellent snorkelling sites, while deeper waters also have some fantastic diving opportunities. The numerous sheltered inlets and coves are vital breeding grounds for four endangered turtles, namely the Leatherback, Olive Ridley, Hawksbill and Green Sea Turtles, so anyone snorkelling or diving is almost guaranteed sightings of these gentle creatures. Also present but less commonly seen is the highly threatened Dugong.

With so much biodiversity it is not surprising that the whole El Nido area has been a protected area since 1984, and more recently it expanded to include a huge region stretching to the town of Taytay on Palawan's opposite, eastern coast.

THE ISLANDS AND BEACHES

Cadlao is probably the best known of the bay's islands, if only because it is the largest and the only island visible from El Nido town. Some other well-known islands include Miniloc and Lagen Islands, sites of luxury resorts owned by the Ten Knots Corporation, which was among the first to promote tourism here. Miniloc has two lovely cliff-encircled lagoons, the Big and Small Lagoons, only the former large enough for a boat, but both perfect for snorkelling and important places for turtle sightings.

Above: A view across the pool at the Lagen Island Resort gives an indication of the low key luxury that is the hallmark of what is one of El Nido's most exclusive island hotels.

Left: Cottages at the Lagen Island Resort nudge up close to the shoreline, themselves almost enveloped in forest vegetation.

Far left: The islands of Bacuit Bay are characterised by their sheer limestone cliffs that tower over the water.

Below: Jagged limestone rocks stand guard just off the main shoreline of Lagen Island.

Mindoro & Palawan

» Other islands include Dilumacad, just south-west of Cadlao (also called Helicopter Island since its distant outline is said to resemble a helicopter), the long, thin Matinloc and the rugged Tapiutan, one of the bay's outermost islands. Almost all these islands have good beaches, though one of the best is Seven Commandos Beach, which is actually on the mainland, but nevethless, like all of El Nido's beaches, is reachable only by boat.

VISITING THE BAY

A great fleet of *bancas* is available for hire in El Nido town or at any of the more remote island resorts around the bay, ready to whisk anyone out to any rock, island or beach, or snorkelling or diving site of their choice. This really is the place to play Robinson Crusoe, for with so many beaches to choose from there will always be one where you can maroon yourself and be completely alone for a few hours (if that is what you want). Kayaking is also possible in the bay's sheltered waters, and a number of places in El Nido town and at the resorts hire out the boats.

When you get tired of the beach and the coral there is always the rainforest to explore, both close to El Nido town and on some of the outer islands. Lagen Island has one of the best rainforest trails, cutting across the island from the Lagen Island Resort. There are also good hiking trails on Cadlao Island and on the mainland close to the town. Never go alone on these trails – always take a guide.

El Nido is rather remote (something that has so far saved it from over-development), sitting on the north-west coast of Palawan, so getting there can be either time-consuming or expensive, but it is definitely worth the effort. Once you arrive there is quite a choice of accommodation, ranging from simple guesthouses mostly in and around El Nido town, to some of Southeast Asia's most exclusive resorts, sitting mainly on their own, secluded islands, tucked away in various corners of Bacuit Bay. Choose whichever suits your budget and style, then relax into El Nido time – that is, very slow, calm and without the need of a watch, phone or computer tablet.

Right: Much of the El Nido landscape is well forested, such as this scene on Lagen Island, showing the fronds of a rattan palm almost enveloping a tall forest tree.

Far right: The beautiful Seven Commandos Beach is one of the most accessible and popular of El Nido's stunning stretches of sand.

The Visayas

The heart of the country, the Visayas are the Philippines' central region, fragmented into hundreds of islands, each with its own distinct personality. The people vary from one island to the next in both temperament and language (or at least dialect), along with their landscapes and economies. For the visitor the swathes of golden coral sand, often set against a backdrop of the ubiquitious coconut palms, are the big attraction. Many of the islands – especially the smaller ones that were originally created by coral reefs, not volcanoes – have beaches that are arguably the best in Southeast Asia. King among these is Boracay, a tiny island off the northern tip of Panay, while other less busy beach areas include Panglao Island, just off the south-west corner of Bohol, Malapascua Island, off the northern tip of Cebu, and Siquijor Island to the south-east of Negros.

Then there is the diving, which is some of the best in East Asia if not the whole of the Pacific region. Many beautiful reefs are easily reached from the beaches, giving even a novice diver the chance to see some fantastic coral gardens, as well as quite an array of reef and sometimes deep-sea fish.

A beautiful white sand bar set against an azure sea is one of the great attractions of the coast at Santa Fe, on Bantayan Island.

Boracay

Without any doubt this is the Philippines' number one destination for visitors, an accolade the island has held for many years, attracting thousands of people from all over the world who come alone, with families, and with small and large tour groups. That so many people come here is remarkable, as the island is tiny, barely 9 km (6 miles) long and just 1 km (½ mile) wide at its narrowest point. It lies off the northernmost tip of Panay, one of the Visayas' main landmasses.

The principal attraction is fabulous White Beach, which is about 5 km (3 miles) long and takes up much of the island's west coast. Its dazzling white sand is fronted by an azure sea and backed by lines of coconut palms, an absolutely quintessential tropical island scene. You might think this would be all such a small island could accommodate, but it packs in several additional beaches, principally Bulabog on the east coast, Diniwid in the north-west and Puka at the northern tip; the last of these is composed almost entirely of millions of tiny seashells.

Above: When it all gets just a bit too much, there are plenty of palm trees to simply collapse under!

Right: Boracay's White Beach is getting a little busy these days for some people's tastes, but it is still one of the most spectacular beaches in the whole of Southeast Asia.

Above: With its dark brown wood and bamboo facings, the buildings of Friday's Resort are instantly recognizable. One of Boracay's earliest upmarket resorts, it remains a firm favourite among many visitors.

» **FROM EARLY BEGINNINGS TO INTERNATIONAL RESORT**

The island was first discovered by backpackers in the late 1970s and early '80s, a time when accommodation was basic and electricity was found only in thunderclouds, but the beach was deserted and pristine. Through the 1980s and '90s development was steady, with new resorts and restaurants springing up along the length of White Beach, but much of the rest of the island was left untouched. Then big corporate money arrived, and a huge golf course and resort complex was built in the north of the island, followed by a luxury Shangri-La resort. Meanwhile, on White Beach, accommodation and restaurants started to change from coconut-wood and *nipa*-thatch construction to glass and concrete, bringing in modern urban chic, at least in terms of architecture.

Boracay's days of rustic simplicity and an empty beach are certainly long gone. They have been replaced by a truly international mainstream visitor attraction, in which not only are the hotel rooms comfortable and completely weather-proof, but also a huge number of restaurants provide a wide range of international cuisines at any time of the day or night. This place is now for the person in search of a stylish holiday, not a challenging, 'wild-frontier' adventure.

One big change that came to the island a couple of years ago is related to the way in which visitors arrive. For many years everyone came in by *banca* to one of three so-called 'boat stations' spread at even distances along the length of White Beach. Now everyone arrives via a constant shuttle of both *bancas* and larger ferries to a purpose-built wharf at Cagban on the island's southernmost tip, the point closest to the Caticlan harbour on the opposite mainland. This trip is then followed by noisy vehicular transport to the hotel, instead of the relaxed sandy stroll from shore to hotel reception that characterized the 'old' Boracay.

Left: When the lack of wind makes windsurfing impossible, there are always souvenirs to be bought, such as these colourful batik lanterns.

Below and far left: Kite-surfing and windsurfing are Boracay's main action sports above the water's surface, concentrated mainly on Bulabog Beach, though when the wind drops away the kites tend to become simply colourful geometric beach art, laid out ready for when the wind may sweep in again.

» ALL THE FUN OF THE SEASIDE

Today paddling, swimming and sunbathing are just three of the more mundane seaside activities, and a vast array of water sports is on offer, from windsurfing and *paraw* sailing (wind-driven *bancas*), to parasailing, snorkelling and scuba diving.

Windsurfing, kite-boarding and wake-boarding are generally concentrated on Bulabog Beach, at least during the tourist high season of the north-east monsoon (November to May), when the winds are onshore. They move over to White Beach, on the opposite side of the island, when the winds switch round to the south-west monsoon (June to September), Boracay's low season. During the high season Boracay hosts a number of international tournaments, including the annual Boracay International Funboard Cup, which has put Boracay firmly on the international windsurfing circuit.

The sailing of *paraw*, which are really quite large *bancas* equipped with far too much sail, is specific to White Beach, with large numbers of these colourful boats for hire concentrated at what remains of the three boat stations – the last vestige of these sites' past role. Many are intended for tour groups to hire en masse, providing sail-powered offshore tours with

locals firmly in charge of the helm. There are also a few smaller *paraw* available for small groups and families, and anyone able to convince the skipper that they really know how to sail a boat might just earn a turn at the helm. In a good breeze these boats are fantastic flying trimarans.

SNORKELLING AND DIVING

Although Boracay is not generally rated as one of the Philippines' top diving spots, there are nevertheless some good opportunities around the island, with a number of healthy reefs in both shallow and deep water, suitable for the beginner and veteran diver alike. Some are also good for snorkelling, including areas around Crocodile and Laurel Islands, both islets off Boracay's south-eastern corner. For experienced divers the star attraction is Yapak, a group of four dive sites off the northern tip that feature a steep, deep, coral-covered wall and provide opportunities to see pelagic fish, such as Barracudas, Giant Trevallies and Dogtooth Tuna.

There is a host of dive operations based along White Beach, so there is plenty of choice. For the novice, Boracay is a great place to learn to dive, as the operators are all well established and experienced, and there are many ideal dive sites.

Left: One of Boracay's many *paraw*, a sailing *banca* with an enormous amount of sail area, hauls up at White Beach to wait for customers to take on a sailing tour of the island.

Above: A shoal of Barracuda seen at Yapak, one of Boracay's deepest and most exciting dive sites, whose deep waters and strong currents are exactly the kind of place for frequent encounters with this predatory species.

Cebu City and Mactan Island

The economic hub of the Visayas, indeed of the whole of the central Philippines, Cebu City is the country's second city, one of its busiest international ports and capital of the island province of Cebu. To the east lies Mactan Island, home to the city's airport and a number of high-end resorts that line the island's south-east coast, as well as the site of one of the country's most significant moments in history.

CEBU CITY

This sprawling metropolis has been an international trading centre for many hundreds of years, long before the Spanish arrived. It traded with other ports all across Southeast Asia, as well as with China and the Middle East. Indeed, when Ferdinand Magellan showed up in April 1521 he was very much the latecomer – the last person to show up to Cebu's international trading party.

Of course Magellan arrived with religion and conquest also on his mind, and although he was initially successful in impressing the locals, he went just a little too far and within a couple of weeks was dead, killed on Mactan at the hands of Lapu-Lapu, the island's chief. In the years since Philippine independence, Lapu-Lapu has been built up as the country's first patriot, and his act of defiance is celebrated on Mactan annually on the anniversary, 27 April.

Following Magellan's death and the subsequent failure of his mission, it would be another 38 years before the Spanish tried again. This time they came under the command of Miguel Lopez de Legazpi, who arrived in Cebu in 1565. He made certain of his takeover by quickly building a harbourside fort (Fort San Pedro, which still stands today) and establishing Spain's first permanent settlement in the Philippines. It was from here that Spain's inexorable takeover of the country began, spreading first to nearby Iloilo and then northwards to Manila and Vigan.

Left: Magellan's Cross, standing in a simple but attractive domed pavilion in the middle of central Cebu City, is said to mark the spot where Ferdinand Magellan planted the first Christian cross on Philippine soil, in April 1521.

Right: At the northern end of Mactan Island stands a modern statue of Lapu-Lapu, the chief of Mactan, who killed Magellan in April 1521.

Far right: Just a few metres from the Lapu-Lapu statue, stands the Magellan Monument, erected here by the Spanish colonial government, and possibly marking the spot where Magellan was killed.

» REMAINS OF THE PAST

Today the old part of Cebu City, known locally as Downtown and not surprisingly close to the port area, is littered with remnants left behind by Legazpi and his men. Nearest to the port is Fort San Pedro, which was built in 1565 and was the first fortification put up by the Spanish in the Philippines. It is an attractive partial ruin set in its own leafy garden and park, a great place in which to wander, relax and ponder.

Further into town is the grandly named Basilica Minore del Santo Niño, a church housing the Philippines' holiest relic, a small Flemish statue of the infant Jesus presented by Magellan to the wife of the Cebu chief Rajah Humabon in 1521. Although the original basilica was built in 1565, today's building dates from the 18th century. A solid stone building, it stood up against war and earthquake until October 2013, when sadly its belfry and part of its façade were demolished by a powerful tremor. Reconstruction will certainly take quite some time.

Almost directly across the road stands the Cebu Metropolitan Cathedral, a relatively modern building by comparison, dating from the 19th century, its white walls a stark contrast to the basilica's forbidding grey stone.

Opposite the city hall stands another of Cebu's important historical monuments, Magellan's Cross (see page 108). A giant cross, a replica of one planted by Magellan but said to contain inside it splinters from the original, it stands inside an attractive rotunda, the domed ceiling of which is adorned with a painting of a group of Filipinos working to plant the cross while Magellan and a few of his men stand by with a priest.

Apart from these sites the old Downtown district contains little of interest, aside from perhaps the bustling Carbon Market. To see the modern city you need to head for the more inland Uptown area.

Right: The grounds of Fort San Pedro, the first permanent structure erected by the invading Spanish under the command of Miguel Lopez de Legazpi in 1565. Today the fort lies in parkland close to Cebu City's main port area.

CEBU CITY AND MACTAN ISLAND

Left and far left: Although Mactan Island is not well endowed with beaches, it does have a fine and very popular stretch of sand near its northern tip at the vast Shangri-La Mactan Resort.

» **UPTOWN CEBU CITY**

This is the city's modern heart, with not much by way of specific visitor attractions except perhaps a couple of interesting Chinese temples, the product of Cebu's large and commercially very successful Chinese community. This is largely an area of highways, office and apartment tower blocks, department stores and huge shopping malls. The last of these are worth dropping into, if only to chill out and escape the traffic. The Ayala Center is arguably one of the biggest and most popular of such malls.

MACTAN ISLAND

Holding itself at arm's length from the city, but nevertheless becoming increasingly urbanized, Mactan is important to visitors for its airport and shoreline resorts. Though it has to be admitted that the beaches here are not particularly fantastic, a few of the resorts do maintain their own private beaches quite well. Top among these is the massive Shangri-La Mactan Resort, resplendent with not only the requisite swimming pools but also a lovely tropical garden, which leads down to a small but nevertheless beautiful beach, from where diving and boating can be organized for those feeling too energetic for the usual sunbathing and swimming.

It is definitely worthwhile visiting one or two of Mactan's guitar workshops, for which the island is rightly famed. Produced mainly around the village of Abuno, Mactan's acoustic guitars are not cheap tourist souvenirs, but musical instruments beautifully hand-crafted using traditional methods and aimed at the serious music market.

Beyond Mactan, to the south-east, lies Olango Island. It is flat and low lying, barely more than a couple of metres above sea level, and a great place to escape the city to some rural tranquillity. Its most important feature is Olango Island Wildlife Sanctuary, which is close to the island's southern tip and is the site of vast sandflats and mangroves. This is a vital part of the East Asia Flyway for tens of thousands of birds migrating annually between northern Asia and Australia, as well as for over-wintering birds from November to February. It is a great place for birdwatchers.

Above: One of the Philippines' millions of coconut palms almost glows a golden colour in the late afternoon sun, seen on Mactan Island.

Cebu's Northern Islands

The long, north–south, pencil-shaped island province of Cebu is capped at its northern end by a cluster of islands, two of which have lovely white-sand beaches and a well-developed set of beach resorts: Bantayan and Malapascua. Until just a few years ago both were completely unknown, but they are now attracting an increasing stream of visitors, to the point that Malapascua at least is becoming a mainstream tourism destination.

The two are very different islands, Bantayan being much larger than Malapascua. Bantayan has a road system and several towns, while Malapascua is barely a couple of kilometres long, criss-crossed with a network of dusty footpaths, each linking up a smattering of simple fishing villages. Bantayan can be reached by car ferry from both Cebu City and Hagnaya, the latter being the nearest town on the Cebu mainland, while Malapascua is reached only by *banca* linking the island with the village of Maya, at

the northern tip of the Cebu mainland. Do not bother trying to take a vehicle to Malapascua.

Both islands are extremely relaxed, easy-going and friendly, the total antidote to the hustle and bustle of Cebu City less than 150 km (90 miles) to the south. Beach relaxation is definitely the name of the game on both islands, backed up by a sprinkling of beachside restaurants, bars and resorts, on Bantayan very low key, but on Malapascua increasingly high-end. Entertainment is very much of the slow, quiet type – don't come to Bantayan or Malapascua for nightclubs and raucous parties. Malapascua doesn't even have mains electricity, relying on a string of generators to keep the resorts powered-up. What Malapascua does have, however, is very good diving, something that was the initial trigger to set the tiny island on the tourism path. To this day, diving continues to be one of Malapascua's main draws, quite apart from its lovely beaches.

Right: On Bantayan Island, Santa Fe's few beachside bars and cafes are still very low-key, relaxed affairs, owned and run mostly by local people, the perfect place to sit back and chill out.

The Visayas

Right: A palm-shaded, thatch-roofed pergola beside
Sugar Beach, a great place to relax.

Far right: Sunrise over a fishing boat and the distant
mainland.

Below right: A stunningly blue sky and a mirror-calm
azure sea, separated by the green and white strip of Alice
Beach, seen from the Santa Fe port.

» **BANTAYAN ISLAND**

Only about 16 km (10 miles) long, Bantayan is a highly rural place with just two principal towns, Santa Fe in the south-east and Bantayan town in the south-west, the latter being the administrative capital. Santa Fe is the main visitor attraction, with beaches and resorts stretching along the coast both north and south of the town's harbour.

SANTA FE

Arriving at Santa Fe from Hagnaya, the moment you step off the ferry you are aware that you have landed in a very different environment from that of mainland Cebu. The sun seems brighter, the sea even bluer; everything moves more slowly, and the air is lightly scented with a mixture of sea salt and blossoms. The tension and the need to rush everywhere quickly fall away, and both your mind and muscles start to relax.

Santa Fe's harbour consists simply of a very long concrete jetty, to which a steady stream of rusty old freighters tie up, bringing and taking away cement, fertilizer and fish, to name just the most obvious. It feels like an unhurried, cumbersome operation, with the loading and unloading being managed purely by teams of men manhandling each sack in turn, the hard work made even more laborious by the heavy tropical air. To anyone used to the sight of a slick container port, this is a throwback to a previous era, lost from the cities and bigger ports, but wholly suited to this island outpost. It sets the mood as you walk down the jetty away from the ferry, introducing the island's slower pace of life, its less 'modern' ways and the fact that this is not just a visitor attraction but a place of work, too.

The town is about 2 km (1¼ miles) to the south, a spacious but simple grid of streets laid out in the south-eastern corner of the island, just where the coast does a sharp right turn from the east coast to the south. It is a quiet, friendly little town almost devoid of traffic, and equipped with the usual government office, school, church and market, plus a cluster of bars and restaurants, mostly close to the beach and catering mainly for visitors.

Above: Having the space and time to relax on an idyllic tropical beach: a couple walk along Sugar Beach's sand bar.

» The majority of the buildings are characterless concrete structures, though many houses have cared-for gardens whose vegetation shades and indeed almost envelopes each house. There are still a few remnants of former times, when houses were wooden, and windows adorned with fretwork and simple carvings, but sadly most of these are now falling into ruin, unloved and uncared-for. The church, on the other hand, is undergoing a huge restoration; a bigger new church is literally being built over and around the existing building, complete with a new domed roof adorned with trumpet-blowing angels.

The beaches start within a short distance of the jetty, on both sides, with Sugar Beach to the south and Alice Beach to the north. They are lined with the usual coconut palms, as well as with a smattering of resorts, all quite small and mostly locally owned. The beaches are long, dazzlingly white strips of sand, Sugar Beach complete with an attractive sandbar that is reachable at low tide. Most of the beach is quiet and undeveloped; apart from the small resorts there is only a cluster of bars and cafes at its closest point to the town, just around the island's southeastern point.

MALAPASCUA ISLAND

In a few short years Malapascua has been transformed from a remote fishermen's island to an important tourism attraction. While fishing villages remain scattered across the island, the visitors congregate at Bounty Beach, which stretches along pretty well the whole of the island's south coast, all 1 km (½ mile) of it. Resorts, many of them increasingly upmarket, line most of the beach, attracting visitors from all over the world.

In the island's south-west corner lies the main village, Logon, which fronts onto Poblacion Beach, the site of a few resorts and arrival point for the *banca* ferries coming from Maya at the northern tip of Cebu. This beach is crowded with *bancas* of one sort or another belonging to local fishermen and meant for visitor transport, as well as with specialized scuba-diving boats.

Top right: The village of Guimbitayan at Malapascua's northwest corner.

Below right: A picturesque detail of a slowly disintegrating wooden house in Santa Fe presents a remnant of times past.

Far right: Bounty Beach along Malapascua's south coast is the quintessential tropical beach, a long strip of soft white sand overhung with coconut palms, plus a regular sprinkling of fishing boats.

Top, far left: Thresher Sharks in Malapascua's waters are a big attraction for divers.

Top, centre left: The vegetation of Malapascua's inland areas includes the occasional jackfruit tree.

Top, left: A young boy learns his trade as a fisherman off the shore of Guimbitayan.

Left: The magnificent and as yet completely undeveloped beach along Malapascua's northern shore.

Above: The lighthouse on Malapascua's west coast is a landmark along any walking tour of the island.

» **DIVING**

Quite apart from the usual beach-bumming, scuba diving is the main attraction here, most especially for trips to see thresher sharks and manta rays over the nearby Monad Shoal. Normally quite rarely seen, here these creatures are relatively common, with regular sightings possible though not guaranteed. Other good diving opportunities include three wreck dives and an area off nearby Gato Island rich in sea snakes. Bounty Beach is home to a number of dive operations, though one of the most well established is at Malapascua Exotic Resort, one of the island's first pioneers and the original discoverer of the thresher shark presence.

EXPLORING THE ISLAND

At only a little more than 2 km (1¼ miles) long, the island can be walked around in just a few hours, something that is best done very early in the morning when the air is still quite cool. It is a pleasant hike through shady trees and woodland, as well as some dry, scrubby vegetation. There are a couple of small beaches along the west coast, until you then come to the lighthouse and a nearby view of the village of Guimbitayan, up in the island's north-west corner, sitting beside two small but attractive beaches.

You can then cut across the island's north coast to the small Bantigue Cove Beach Resort, nestling in the island's north-east corner and on a hillside above a small, shingly beach. Between here and Guimbitayan, however, stretches the most spectacular white-sand beach – apparently still unnamed – which is deserted apart from a few fishing boats, its waters a stunning aquamarine and azure.

Dumaguete and Beyond

Lying in the south-east corner of Negros, one of the Visaya's main islands, Dumaguete is a pleasant town, home to Silliman University, originally the USA's first private university in Asia. Although there is not a great deal specifically to see in Dumaguete itself, the surrounding area is of great interest, and highly varied at that.

THE CITY

Dumaguete is in essence a small provincial city, but one made remarkably cosmopolitan and outward-looking by the presence of Silliman University. The university campus is largely integrated with the town, characterized by a number of American colonial buildings that lend a sophisticated architectural streak, as well as several very attractive tree-lined avenues. The city centre is quite a compact grid of streets not far from the main Silliman campus and centred around Quezon Park.

Opposite the park stands the attractive Dumaguete Cathedral, dating from 1885 but with a façade added in 1936, complete with statues of Sts Matthew, Mark, Luke and John on individual columns fronting the main entrance. These lend the cathedral an incongruous Greco-Roman appearance that is at odds with its baroque Hispanic façade. Close by stands Dumaguete's only truly historic monument, the 18th-century Bell Tower, all that remains of the original cathedral.

Dumaguete's cosmopolitan feel is expressed by the presence of a significant number of overseas students, as well as a sense of the culture of learning, as illustrated by Dumaguete's museums, the most prominent of which is the harbourside Anthropology Museum and Centre for the Study of Philippine Living. Further inland, at the northern end of the Silliman campus, is Centrop, a small zoo and breeding centre for some of Negros's endangered endemic species, including the Visayan Spotted Deer and the Visayan Warty Pig. No matter how far you explore into Negros's remaining forests, the chances of seeing either of these in the wild are extremely slim, so Centrop represents just about the only chance to get close to either.

A few blocks over from the cathedral and running southwards from the port is a pleasant shoreline promenade. It is rather quiet and nondescript in the daytime, but in the evening the many bars and cafes that line the promenade turn it into a huge outdoor entertainment zone.

This is definitely the place to come to both relax and party with the locals, at the weekend especially the whole promenade strip is suffused with a warm and hospitable atmosphere, helped along by some truly great seafood restaurants and live music.

Right: Spinner dolphins swim ahead of a boat.

Far right: Seen from the bow of a boat, a group of Spinner dolphins cuts across right in front.

Above: Two young girls stand in the bow of a boat, keeping a lookout for dolphin pods in the Tanon Strait.

» DOLPHIN WATCHING IN THE TANON STRAIT

North of Dumaguete, the town of Bais sits on the shores of the Tanon Strait, a narrow and very deep stretch of water (reaching in excess of 500 metres/1,640 feet deep) that separates Negros from Cebu to the east. These sheltered waters are rich in marine life, and are renowned for the number of dolphins and – to a lesser extent – whales that can be seen here, making Bais absolutely the place to come for dolphin watching.

According to the environmental organization Greenpeace, the Tanon Strait is home to 11 of the 25 cetacean species found in Philippine waters, making this stretch of water crucial to Southeast Asian marine conservation. Despite this, oil exploration drilling has been allowed in the Strait, the submarine noise from which is believed to be driving the whales and dolphins away. It is an issue that has reached the Philippines' highest courts.

For the time being, at least, dolphin numbers remain good, enabling Bais's *banca* owners to make a worthwhile living running dolphin-watching tours from both the town's main harbour and from the village of Manjuyod about 15 km (9 miles) further north. The best time of day is very early in the morning, when the usually calm, windless conditions make it easier to spot dolphin pods from a distance. At this time, quite a fleet of *bancas* can usually be seen tracking any number of groups of dolpins out in the strait.

Although whales can be seen here, they are far less common than dolphins, and even when present usually consist of only the smaller species, such as Pilot Whales. These can usually be found in small groups, whose black bulbous heads can be seen bobbing up and down in the water as they 'periscope' to view their surroundings.

The most commonly seen dolphin species are Risso's and Spinner. While the former seem to be rather shy, frequently diving when approached by a boat, the Spinner dolphins appear to be generally quite at ease, happy to ride along on the boats' bow waves, ducking, diving and weaving just ahead of the bow, frequently leaping clear out of the water. The dolphins move at such incredible speeds (how can the single flick of a tail cause such amazing acceleration?) that it is almost impossible to predict where they will come up next, a group that one minute was right under your bow, the next is over a hundred metres (300 feet) away. Watching these amazing animals is an exhilarating experience.

Left: The rugged landscape of Mt Talinis, also known as Cuernos de Negros, its lower slopes cleared for agriculture, its upper slopes still forested.

» INTO THE MOUNTAINS

Dumaguete is backed by a high range of mountains, which are the site of some of southern Negros' last remaining stands of healthy lowland rainforest and the place to see some really big trees, the dipterocarps (the name referring to their two-winged fruit). The highest of the mountains is Mt Talinis, also known as Cuernos de Negros, the Horns of Negros, after its twin peaks, which are 1,870 m (6,134 ft) high. There is a trail to the top, making for a steep, sweaty hike that can be completed in a single day.

The mountain sits on the southern edge of Balinsasayao Twin Lakes Natural Park, at just over 8,000 ha (20,000 acres) protecting the best of the remaining forest. The Twin Lakes themselves, consisting of Lakes Balinsasayao and Danao, lie on the park's northern side at an altitude of just under 900 m (2,900 ft), deep inside old volcano craters and surrounded by forested mountain peaks. Both areas are visitor attractions offering boating, fishing, hiking and birdwatching (the park is known for its diversity of forest-bird species), and are accessible via a rough road from Sibulan, a coastal village between Dumaguete and Bais. Nearby, at the park's entrance, is a third lake, the smaller Kabalin-an Lake, which contains a small number of swamp-forest trees and is backed by steep mountain slopes cloaked in forest.

On the lower slopes of Mt Talinis, south-west of Dumaguete, sits the town of Valencia, the starting point for both trails to the summit and hikes to a number of waterfalls. Most prominent among these is the spectacular, 30 m (98 ft) high Casaroro Falls, which thunders down a vertical cliff into a natural pool before pouring off into a powerful stream. The falls and stream are set in a very steep, narrow valley reached by over 300 steps and a difficult walk over boulders upstream for a few hundred metres, with the forests of Mt Talinis towering above. The sight of the falls makes the strenuous hike all worthwhile.

THE SOUTHERN COAST

Along the coast south of Dumaguete are a number of attractive beaches and resorts, particularly at Dauin. Offshore sits tiny, rocky Apo Island, the site of some of the best and most exciting scuba diving in the Philippines. Deep, clear water, steep drop-offs and long-term effective protection have ensured the presence of fabulous corals, gigantic sponges and superb fish life that are hard to beat. Dive trips to Apo can be organized through several dive operations in Dumaguete or at the Dauin resorts, while *banca* trips to Apo Island itself (site of a fishing village, a small resort and a modest beach) can be organized at Malatapay, a town further south from Dauin.

Siquijor

Right: Beautiful Paliton Beach is one of many lovely, still unspoiled beaches scattered along Siquijor's coast.

Centre right: The Danish Lagoon Resort, owned by a Danish couple who live on the site, is a small, upmarket resort just outside San Juan.

Far right: Feeling a little nostalgic, perhaps, a perfect replica of Copenhagen's Mermaid statue has been created beside the shore at the Danish Lagoon.

Below right: A lone tree stands on a clifftop near San Juan, silhouetted against the dusk sky.

Isla del Fuego, the 'Island of Fire' the early Spanish conquistadors called it, so named either because they were so overcome by the brilliance of the huge numbers of fireflies lighting up the island's trees at night, or because – according to local legend – the island rose from the sea during a violent thunderstorm. You can take your pick as to which to believe. The former is rather more likely, but even the latter may have a touch of truth to it. The island is certainly composed of the remains of a raised coral reef – huge shells have been found in its fields and even on its highest hills, more than 500 m (1,600 ft) above sea level – but the up-thrusting process presumably took millennia rather than the course of a single storm.

What is certain is that the island is fantastically beautiful, to this day almost completely off anyone's beaten track, surprisingly thinly populated, very rural and largely undeveloped. The main road around the island is tarmacked, there are motorized vehicles on it (though rather few), there is electricity, mobile phones will work, there are places to stay and you can buy certain American soft drinks. But that seems to be about it for 'development' – and there seem to be plenty of people who are happy to have things stay that way.

MYSTICISM AND HEALING

Siquijor's position out of the Philippine mainstream is quite probably linked to its reputation as a place of sorcery, magic and mysticism, a reputation that has led to it being shunned by many Filipinos, making them reluctant to go anywhere near the island. It is certainly true that Siquijor has been, and continues to be today, a home to faith and spiritual healers who use a mix of incantations and herbal remedies in a host of treatments, but it is hard to imagine that this amounts to any kind of evil magic.

Above: The inviting, cool waters of the spring in the centre of San Juan town.

SIQUIJOR

Top right: A mass of floats makes for an attractive pattern in a coiled and piled-up fishing net on Paliton Beach.

Below right: A girl holds up a flying fish, for sale on Paliton Beach.

Far right: Coconut palms hang over the beautiful beach at San Juan.

» Whether fear of possible spirits is the cause or not, the island is – almost uniquely in the Philippines – devoid of crowds, heavy traffic, pollution and souvenir touts, quite amazing for a place whose 100-km (62-mile) coastline is ringed with some of the most sparklingly pristine beaches in the entire country.

BEACH LIFE

Probably the longest and most lovely of Siquijor's beaches is that at the little town of San Juan on the south-west coast. It comprises several kilometres of dazzling white sand, as usual backed by coconut palms and fronted by a calm azure sea. This is where you find the main concentration of the island's resorts, most of which are quite small and relatively simple; all are very quiet and easy-going. To the north-west, beyond the western end of San Juan Beach and close to Siquijor's westernmost point, stretches Paliton Beach, an incredibly attractive place still very much the preserve of the local fishermen.

San Juan itself is a friendly little town, barely more than a single street, with at its centre a natural spring pool. This is usually populated by the local children, who spend most of their time cooling off in its fresh, clear water. Resorts stretch along the beach on either side of the town, with a bar and scuba-diving operation between the beach and the market.

A second beach area, complete with resorts, sits on the opposite side of the island, close to its northern tip and around the village of Sandugan, while a small beach that is popular with local residents is on the east coast at Salagdoong. Following the road along the north-west coast between Sandugan and San Juan, you come to two small towns, Larena and Siquijor town, the former a working port, the latter the island's capital. Although the latter is not officially a port, most of the ferries coming to Siquijor from the surrounding islands of Negros, Cebu and Bohol arrive here. Siquijor town really does not feel like any kind of capital, but seems rather to be a sleepy little village that is mostly rather diffuse and scattered. A small grid of streets that constitute the town centre lies up a hill and some way from the ferry harbour, the historic Spanish church dedicated to St Francis of Assisi stands between the two, and housing areas are hidden among vegetation distributed thinly and widely. It is most definitely a very laid-back, unhurried kind of place.

SIQUIJOR

Left: A small part of the lovely Cambugahay Falls, seen shortly before sunset. This is a popular swimming hole for locals, the cool water streaming down from Siquijor's inland hills.

Below: The town of Lazi, on Siquijor's south coast, is home to the huge San Isidro Labrador Church, adjacent to what was once the Philippines' largest convent.

» HEADING INLAND

East of San Juan is the town of Lazi, home to the 19th-century San Isidro Labrador Church and a former convent, claimed to have been the largest in the Philippines at one time. The church and convent stand among huge verdant trees, separated from the main part of town by a steep hill, with the town down by the seashore, the church and convent on the hilltop.

A couple of kilometres inland and in foothills rising towards the island's hilly interior are the rather small but very attractive Cambugahay Falls, set in a narrow, forested valley, a popular swimming place among local people. Continuing away from the coast, a steep and twisting road network leads all the way to Mt Bandilaan, at 557 metres (1,827 ft) Siquijor's highest peak. Here you find forested Bandilaan Mountain View Park, the venue every Easter for Siquijor's Healing Festival, when the island's traditional healers come together to produce concoctions made from ingredients gathered in the wild every Friday during Lent. Nearby are a butterfly sanctuary and several explorable caves, as well as a network of hiking trails.

Siquijor is a lovely, quiet place, absolutely created for those wanting to step out of the mad rush of the so-called modern world. Do not come here if you want flashing lights, loud music and fast cars.

Bohol: the Mainland

A world away from the crowded streets of Manila and Cebu City, the lush rural island of Bohol is a fascinating place, justifiably attracting a steadily growing number of visitors. Panglao Island, off the south-west coast, is Bohol's principal attraction, but the mainland is gradually pulling in greater attention and people are starting to explore its hilly interior.

Originally only the oddly shaped hillocks comprising the Chocolate Hills attracted attention, marketed as the quintessential Philippine landscape, their image used in advertising to promote the Philippines as a whole. Thankfully the Chocolate Hills are increasingly just a starter.

A COLONIAL HISTORY

Bohol had a rather chequered history in its relationship with the Spanish, starting in 1565 when Bohol's chieftain, Rajah Sikatuna, signed a blood compact with Miguel Lopez de Legazpi. Two centuries later the Boholanos were successful in throwing out the Spanish, gaining effective independence for the island that lasted until the early years of the 19th century.

In the years between, Spanish priests were very busy putting up a number of impressive churches, buildings that survive as some of the Philippines' most historic and best-preserved colonial relics. Today a Boholano church tour would take in churches at Loon, Baclayon and Loboc, to name just the most famous. Baclayon Church, sitting on the seashore just to the east of the provincial capital Tagbilaran, was at one time thought to be Bohol's oldest church. However, apparently its estimated date of construction has been pushed back to the early years of the 18th century, allowing one of its neighbours into the number one slot. That honour belongs to San Pedro Church, at nearby Loboc, which is believed to have been built in about 1602. All the churches are built in the 'Earthquake Baroque' style, with San Pedro being an attractive example of this. Sadly, some of its massive walls and façade collapsed in the October 2013 earthquake. Reconstruction will take quite some time.

Above: Floating restaurants on the Loboc River, surrounded by lush vegetation in the Boholano interior, near Loboc.

» BOHOLANO LANDSCAPES

San Pedro Church sits beside the Loboc River, directly opposite the start and finish points for what must be mainland Bohol's number two visitor attraction: boat tours along the Loboc River. The tours follow the river through a lovely forested and agricultural landscape, geared to the needs of large tour groups, leading the boats to be big and crowded, complete with loud music and karaoke. Not my kind of thing, but clearly others like it.

To the north-east and en route to the Chocolate Hills lies the town of Bilar. The town itself is unremarkable, but just to the east lies Logarita Pool, a great place for a refreshing dip. The pool sits right on the fringe between hilly forest and pancake-flat farmland, the forest marking the edge of Rajah Sikatuna National Park, roughly 9,000 ha (22,200 acres) of protected rainforest. The park, the entrance of which is close to Logarita, is well known for its bird life and attracts birdwatching groups from around the world, but it is also home to a number of mammals, including flying lemurs, fruit bats, very cute tarsiers (see page 139) and Long-tailed Macaques. There are some partially signposted footpaths through the forest, exploration of which can be an adventure. Bird life is usually best seen early in the morning or late afternoon, but when it comes to mammals only the macaques are likely to make themselves visible.

The Chocolate Hills lie further north-east of here, close to the town of Carmen. Consisting of a series of softly rounded hillocks, the 'chocolate' part largely refers to the colour they tend to go towards the end of the prolonged dry season. The vast majority of visitors see the hills from the only developed hilltop viewpoint, but there is nothing to stop adventurous types who want a different angle from heading into the landscape to explore it for themselves.

Right: The renowned Chocolate Hills, a mass of rounded hillocks, near the town of Carmen in Bohol's interior.

Far Left: Early morning calm at Anda White Beach Resort, at Anda in the southeast of Bohol.

Left: A beachside villa of a more prosaic nature, beside the beach at Anda town.

» **A TASTE OF FOREST WILDLIFE**

The Philippine Tariser (*Carlito syrichta*) is one of only three genera (or species groups) in the world, the other two living in Borneo, Suluwesi and eastern Sumatra. Barely 5 cm (2 in) long, but with a tail at least three times this, the tarsier is the world's smallest primate. It is also impossibly cute, with huge, pleading eyes that seem to fill most of its face. Restricted to the southernmost parts of the Philippines, including Bohol, the Philippine Tarsier is, of course, in trouble, though in Bohol there is a project to help pull it through – the Tarsier Research and Development Center – centred close to the village of Corella, north of Tagbilaran. A visit here represents the best chance to see this tiny creature, via a guided tour around a small, enclosed piece of forest in which are kept a number of tarsiers. All you will see in there is wall-to-wall trees, but your guide will know exactly how to find the tarsiers, displaying an uncanny ability to point them out among the vegetation, usually barely a metre above your head.

BACK TO THE BEACH

Mainland Bohol has few beach resorts (at present, anyway), but out on an eastern peninsula is Anda, which is increasingly billed as an alternative to the beaches of Panglao Island. Several kilometres of white sand line the coast around the village of Anda, though it is still little known and generally lightly visited. As a result this is an extremely quiet place to head for, complete with some very peaceful, comfortable resorts.

Being a coralline limestone area, Anda's landscape is riddled with caves, some of which are easily accessible and close to the resorts. Some contain early remains of human habitation going back thousands of years, and one of the most important is located on an offshore islet and contains prehistoric rock paintings. It is for these finds that Anda is often thought of as the cradle of Boholano civilisation.

Above: Nature's mascot for Bohol, the Tarsier, a tiny primate barely 8 cm (3 in) long (excluding the much longer tail) that is native to the island.

Bohol: Panglao Island

Just off Bohol's south-west coast and linked to the mainland by a short bridge is Panglao Island, one of the Philippines' most popular beach areas and Bohol's main visitor attraction. White-sand beaches are dotted around most of the island's coast, though several are privately owned, integral parts of upmarket resorts such as Eskaya Beach Resort and Bohol Beach Club. More accessible beaches include Bikini, Dumaluan (both on the south coast), and Momo Beaches (on the north coast), while by far the most developed and best known of the open beaches is Alona Beach, in Panglao's south-west, part of the barangay (or village) of Tawala.

ALONA AND OFFSHORE

Originally this strip of white sand largely attracted divers, who were drawn by the area's fantastic undersea world, but today the beach is lined with resorts and restaurants that cater to a host of needs and types of visitor, with the resorts steadily creeping upmarket and increasing in size. The beach is getting quite busy these days, but it is still a great place in which to chill out and to use as a base from which to explore the island and surrounding waters.

A crowd of *bancas* is moored offshore, ready to whisk anyone off on any kind of tour or to any of the many dive sites nearby. For non-divers among the most popular are early-morning trips to watch dolphins, which are regularly seen a couple of kilometres or so to the south, followed by a visit to Virgin Beach, a beautiful tidal sandbar off Panglao's western tip. Perhaps one of the most popular spots to head for is Balicasag Island, about 6 km (4 miles) from Alona, a gorgeous coral island completely ringed by a dazzlingly white beach, which can be walked around in about an hour. Be sure to take plenty of water if you decide to do this as there is little shade.

Balicasag also happens to be one of the most fabulous dive sites in the whole of the Philippines, this one island alone being responsible for attracting many of the divers who come to Panglao. Protected as a marine sanctuary, the island is surrounded by sheer submarine cliffs that drop down to depths of over 50 m (160 ft). They are covered in a huge array of soft and hard corals, and their waters contain great shoals of pelagic fish such as trevally and barracuda, as well as occasional sharks.

There are plenty of other great dive sites in the area – such places as Napaling and Duljo Point, off Panglao's north and north-west coast, and Cervera Shoal and Pamilacan Island, a few kilometres south-east of Alona. All have healthy coral and some superb marine life – this consists mostly of reef species, but at some sites, such as Duljo Point, there is a variety of deep-sea fish.

Above right: The white sand beach and azure sea, both of which completely surround Balicasag Island.

Below right: A Green Turtle on the steep wall off the north coast of Panglao Island.

» **INLAND PANGLAO**

Most of the attention on Panglao is focused on the
coastline, but there are a few things that are worth
heading inland for. East of Alona is Tarsier Botanika, a
superb tropical garden carved out of the scrubby
coralline limestone landscape, complete with ponds, a
reclining Buddha (a very Thai touch) and a rather
exclusive restaurant with clifftop sea views.

Sadly, in October 2013, the Visayas, and in particular
Bohol, was struck by a massive earthquake that killed
over 200 people, made hundreds of thousands
homeless and devastated some of the country's most
important historic monuments. One such was the
Church of Our Lady of the Assumption, in the town of
Dauis, whose interior was superbly and uniquely
decorated. Much of its façade was destroyed.

With this exception, Panglao escaped relatively lightly,
though the same cannot be said for mainland Bohol.
With the epicentre directly beneath Bohol, close to the
village of Sagbayan, the damage to lives, roads and
buildings was immense. Several historic churches were
badly damaged, including those at Baclayon and Loboc
(see page 135). Bohol has been badly hurt. But it is still
beautiful, and in the coming years it will recover.

Right: The lush pool garden at Charts Resort, Alona Beach.

Far right: A very Thai-looking, reclining Buddha statue,
complete with lotus pond, at the beautiful Tarsier Botanika
garden, near Alona Beach.

Mindanao

The Philippines' southern landmass and the country's second largest island, much of Mindanao remains rather lightly explored by visitors, despite its superb mountainous landscape and rugged coastline. The most accessible and visited areas are in the north and east, and although many parts of the south and west, such as Zamboanga and Dipolog, are also really worth visiting, they struggle against the perception that they are not safe due to unrest in neighbouring areas, such as Sulu and Basilan.

Northern Mindanao is blessed with two of the most lovely jewels in the whole of the Philippines, Siargao Island off the north-east coast, and teardrop-shaped Camiguin Island off the north coast. The latter is a mountainous volcanic island ringed with black-sand beaches, a place simply to relax on and forget about the world and all its troubles.

Siargao, though very laid-back, is more about action: surfing action in particular. Discovered in the 1990s by a handful of wandering Australian surfers, the Pacific surf that booms along this island's eastern shore now has Siargao firmly in the international surfing network. And for non-surfers there are even some idyllic golden beaches.

The simple, but attractive boardwalk that makes life easy for surfers wanting to get out to the action on the reef at Cloud Nine, Siargao Island, one of Mindanao's leading attractions.

Siargao Island

The largest island in a mini-archipelago that is protected as a national park, called rather clumsily Siargao Island Protected Landscapes and Seascapes, Siargao is slowly emerging to become arguably Mindanao's main visitor destination. Its growing popularity is largely down to the surf that sweeps in along the island's east coast, particularly from July to September, when typhoons passing by further north set up some great swells. Those waves have become internationally renowned, drawing in avid surfers from around the world. Increasingly, non-surfers are also arriving, attracted in part by a desire to try their hand at the boarding, but also by the island's relaxed culture and golden beaches.

CLOUD NINE

The action centres on Siargao's south-east corner, at a reef and bay that the first Australian surfers to arrive in the 1990s dubbed Cloud Nine, so overwhelmed were they by the perfection of the waves. Today the vast majority of Siargao's steadily growing number of resorts is concentrated here, lined up along a dusty track that parallels the shore.

That shore is a mixture of sandy beach, coconut palms and jagged coralline rocks, with the surfing a couple of hundred metres offshore along a fringing reef. In the early days surfers had a long, tiring paddle to reach the waves, but now life is made easy by a rickety but picturesque boardwalk that allows the surfers to jump straight into the waves, and also provides a grandstand for spectators.

As is the case with most surfing centres, the laid-back surfer-dude culture is alive and well here, adding to Siargao's pre-existing and naturally relaxed 'mañana' lifestyle. It is no good for anyone to bring their urban pace of life here – that should be left behind at the airport or ferry pier. Anything you plan to do should be carried out slowly and quietly.

Above right: A rocky, palm-lined shore close to Cloud Nine, on Siargao's south-east coast.

Below right: A surfer hits the action at Cloud Nine.

Far right: The simple beach at Cloud Nine, just south of the start of the surfers' boardwalk.

» Cloud Nine's nearest 'metropolis' is the ramshackle little town of General Luna (universally abbreviated to GL by anyone on the island for more than 30 minutes), a few kilometres down the coast to the south. It consists of a small grid of streets, a few shops where groceries can be picked up and a huge church. The town backs onto a beach that is lined with fishing boats and where pigs and chickens are reared by the local fishermen. A long jetty reaches out from the beach, from where *bancas* can be hired or ferries (usually just *bancas* running on a regular schedule) caught to outer islands.

EXPLORING SIARGAO

With most of Siargao's roads now sealed, exploring the island beyond Cloud Nine and GL is relatively easy, usually by hired van or a *habal-habal* (a motorcycle taxi). The latter is one of the great innovations of many parts of rural Philippines, a motorbike with a driver providing quick and cheap rides to almost anywhere. On Siargao it usually even comes complete with a somewhat rickety canopy

somehow attached to the bike, very effectively keeping the midday sun at bay. The *habal-habal* can, however, be excruciatingly painful, especially for anyone not used to riding a motorbike. This is particularly the case when three of four people are crammed onto the one and only seat, and most especially when large parts of the trip are along rather rough, bumpy roads, even if these are sealed, as they frequently are across much of Siargao.

Whatever form of transport you take, much of the journey will be through Siargao's inland areas, a mix of plains and low, rolling hills, covered mainly with rather scrubby forest and intermittent farmland, scenic enough but not really of any great interest. One of the main points to head for is the town of Del Carmen, on the west coast, the starting point for *banca* explorations of the vast mangrove swamp that lies off here. It is the largest in Mindanao and is still home to the enormous Saltwater Crocodile – though you would be very lucky (or unlucky, depending on your point of view) to see one.

Right: The view from the bow of a *banca* as it coasts through the calm waters of the vast mangrove swamp that lies around Del Carmen, on Siargao's north-west coast.

» Near the island's northernmost tip are the Tak-Tak Falls, attractive when they are running well – which they frequently do not during the drier times of the year. During the wet season (November to January), the falls cascade down a sheer cliff into a large swimming pool shaded by forest trees.

Nearby and around the villages of Burgos and Santa Monica are some spectacular beaches, which are arguably among the best in the Philippines. Here, blindingly white coralline sand overhung by coconut palms stretches for miles alongside an unbelievable turquoise and azure sea, yet there is hardly a person on the beaches, and barely even a single resort to be seen. This is still very much the preserve of the local fishermen, along with their forever playing children, who have the world's perfect and most heaven-sent playground (without, of course, being aware of it).

BEYOND SIARGAO

To the south of Siargao is a host of smaller islands that are easily reached by hired *banca* from both Cloud Nine and GL. The nearest is tiny Guyam Islet, which is barely more than a sandbar with a few coconut palms and is a good place for snorkelling. Beyond this lies Dako, a much larger island that is home to a fishing community and is lined by another stunning beach. To the west is Bucas Grande Island, a lightly inhabited island, the site of some still well-preserved lowland rainforest and home to Sohoton Cave, which can be at least partially explored at low tide.

Left: A beachside hut that the locals use for chilling out in the evenings, beside Santa Monica beach.

Far left: The fabulous and completely undeveloped beach at Santa Monica, still the territory purely of local children and fishermen.

Camiguin Island

This island lying off Mindanao's north coast, between the cities of Butuan and Cagayan de Oro, is one of the Philippines' best-kept secrets. A mountainous island less than 25 km (15 miles) long, it has no fewer than five volcanoes, though only one is presently active, Mt Hibok-Hibok, which last erupted in 1951.

There is little to do here and that is part of the attraction; it is another place to just step out of the maelstrom of the modern world, to stop and take a deep breath for a while. Moreover, in a country famed for friendliness Camiguin is king, renowned even among Filipinos for its friendly people. The welcome is calm, quiet and reassuring, the smile warm and sincere. For foreigners used to hearing 'Hey, Joe!' yelled out to them in many Philippine streets (though admittedly much less often now than used to be the case), it comes as a great relief on Camiguin to hear instead the call 'Hey, friend!' Even the island's name has been taken to have a positive meaning – some claim that 'Camiguin' is simply a transliteration of the English 'Come again!', though personally I think that is stretching credibility a touch too far.

EXPLORING CAMIGUIN

Another of Camiguin's attractions is that in this high-speed world, getting there takes a bit of planning and time, and it is often perceived to be remote and inaccessible. It is, in fact, quite easily reached by ferry, usually via the island's main port, at Benoni on the south-east coast. The most frequent service is that between Benoni and Balingoan 60 minutes away on the mainland. Less frequent fast ferries run to and from Cagayan de Oro, and to and from Jagna on the south coast of Bohol. Camiguin does have a small airport, but services are at best on-again, off-again, linking the island – when flights are running – with Cebu.

Above: A tricycle, one of the most common forms of public transport on Camiguin Island, this colourful one seen in countryside near Mambajao, the island's capital.

Right: A small fishing banca drawn up on White Island, a sand bar lying off Camiguin's northern coast, with the mountainous main island as a backdrop.

Mindanao

» Once you have made it to Camiguin, most of the resorts are concentrated in the north of the island, in particular around the villages of Agoho and Yumbing. Here the shore is lined with black-sand beaches populated by fishermen and their boats, which head out mostly in the evenings to catch large tuna, especially in the months October to December. Both shy and friendly, the fishermen are very approachable and always willing to talk about their work and to show off their catch.

Admittedly, black sand is usually considered a poor cousin in comparison to yellow or dazzling coralline white sand, so Camiguin is unlikely ever to attract hordes of beach-goers. However, some white sand is to be found at White and Mantigue Islands, the former nothing more than a rather small sandbar off the north coast, the latter an islet to the south-east. White Island does attract quite a number of visitors these days, who travel out in *bancas* from Yumbing to sunbathe and swim, and to admire the wonderful views back to Camiguin. There is also good diving to

be had around both White Island and Mantigue, as well as at a number of sites along Camiguin's coast, such as Old Volcano, a submarine scene of lava flows and volcanic boulders harbouring a wide variety of large and small marine life. Several of the resorts at Agoho and Yumbing offer diving trips.

Everywhere around Camiguin the island's volcanism dominates and moulds much of its life and attractions. Its relatively gentle coastline soon climbs ever more steeply into a mountainous interior. A whole chain of peaks towers high above the sea, the lower slopes covered with coconut groves and carefully terraced rice paddies, the higher-up areas cloaked in deep green rainforest. The peaks themselves are usually lost from sight, buried in a heavy blanket of cloud. The highest are the twin peaks of Mambajao and Timpoong in the island's centre, which come in at over 1,600 m (5,200 ft) high. Hibok-Hibok, in the north-west, though the island's only active volcano, reaches the lesser height of 1,320 m (4,330 ft).

Above: A detail of a mass of hooks being prepared on a long-line by a fisherman at Agoho.

Top: Camiguin's agricultural landscape consists of fields of emerald green rice, seen here near Mambajao.

Right: Fishermen sorting the early morning catch from their net, on the beach at Agoho, on the north coast.

» All these mountains are excruciatingly steep and rugged, and few people bother to climb them, but for the bold and energetic there are plenty of guides available and willing to lead the way – no one should ever try to climb these mountains without one.

Most mortals prefer to enjoy the scenery around the feet of these giants, getting around using a combination of colourful *jeepneys* and motorized tricycles. These mainly work out of the island's attractive capital, Mambajao, which is located on the north coast. *Jeepneys* operate regular services between the towns, and both forms of travel can be readily hired for tours.

For me the most spectacular of the inland sights is the magnificent Katibawasan Falls, a 70 m (230 ft) ribbon of cascading water thundering down a cliff amid verdant rainforest straight into a pool, on the eastern slopes of Mt Hibok-Hibok. It is a popular spot for the locals, who come here to cool off. Another lovely place nearby that the locals enjoy is Ardent Hot Springs, which is enveloped in a cooling rainforest canopy and directly benefits from being on an active volcano. It is not the island's only hot spring, there being another on the north-west coast at Tangub, a completely undeveloped tidal hot spring that is largely submerged at high tide.

Further round the west coast from Tangub, near the village of Bonbon, the slopes of the Old Camiguin Volcano have been turned into a series of steps consisting of life-size statues depicting Stations of the Cross. Offshore stands a huge cross marking the site of a submerged cemetery that sank into the sea during an earthquake in 1871. Other attractions along this west-coast road include the little-visited Tuwasan Falls and the Santo Niño Cold Springs, both near the southwestern town of Catarman.

Left, above: The forest-enclosed Ardent Hot Springs is divided up into a series of pools and cascading streams, all protected under leaf-catching nets.

Left, below: A family enjoys Ardent's relaxing waters.

Far left: The fantastic Katibawasan Falls thunders down a cliff at the foot of Mt Hibok-Hibok, Camiguin's currently active volcano.

Accommodation Guide

Here is a brief list of places to stay in the locations described in this book. Note that the international telephone code for the Philippines is +63.

LUZON

Banaue Hotel and Youth Hostel
Ilogue, Banaue, Mountain province
Tel: (074) 386 4088

Island Tropic Hotel
Boulevard St, Barangay Lucap, Alaminos City, Pangasinan 2404
Tel: (075) 696 9405
info@islandtropichotel.com
www.islandtropichotel.com

Kapuluan Vista Resort
Sitio Baniaran, Barangay Balaoi, Pagudpud, Ilocos Norte 2919
Tel: 0920 952 2528 (mobile phone)
kapuluan_vista_resort@yahoo.com
www.kapuluanvistaresortand restaurant.com

Little Surfmaid Resort
170 Urbiztondo, San Juan, La Union 2514
Tel: (072) 888 5528
Email: surfmaid@gmail.com
Web: www.littlesurfmaidresort.com

The Manor at Camp John Hay
Loakan Rd, Baguio City, Benguet 2600
Tel: (074) 424 0931
Email: reservations@campjohnhay.ph
Web: www.campjohnhay.ph

Sagada Homestay
Ato Patay, Sagada, Mountain province
Tel: 0919 702 8380 (mobile phone)
sagadahomestay@yahoo.com

Traders Hotel
3001 Roxas Boulevard, Pasay City, Metro Manila 1305
Tel: (02) 708 4888
thm@tradershotels.com
www.tradershotels.com

Villa Angela
26 Quirino Boulevard, Vigan, Ilocos Sur
Tel: (077) 722 2914
villangela.heritage@gmail.com
www.villangela.com

MINDORO

La Laguna Beach Club
Big La Laguna Beach, Puerto Galera, Mindoro Oriental
Tel: (043) 287 3179
lalaguna@llbc.com.ph
www.llbc.com.ph

PALAWAN

Asturias Hotel
South National Highway, Tiniguiban, Puerto Princesa, Palawan
Tel: (048) 433 9744
palawansales@asturiashotel.ph
www.asturiashotel.ph

Lagen Island Resort
El Nido, Palawan
Contact the Manila office:

Ten Knots Development Corporation, 18/F BA Lepanto Building, 8747 Paseo de Roxas, Makati, Metro Manila 1226
Tel: (02) 902 5980
holiday@elnidoresorts.com
www.elnidoresorts.com

THE VISAYAS

Anda White Beach Resort
Sitio Dagohoy, Barangay Bacong, Anda, Bohol 6311
Tel: 0917 700 0507 (mobile phone)
cornelis@andabeachresort.com
www.andabeachresort.com

Charts Resort
Tawala, Alona Beach, Panglao, Bohol 6340
Tel: (038) 502 8918
info@charts-alona.com
www.charts-alona.com

The Danish Lagoon Restaurant and Beach Resort
HC Andersen's Blvd, Paliton, San Juan, Siquijor 6227
Tel: 0908 627 0975 (mobile phone)
info@thedanishlagoon.com
www.thedanishlagoon.com

Discovery Shores Boracay
Station 1, Balabag, Boracay Island, Malay, Aklan 5608
Tel: (036) 288 4500
rsvn@discovery.com.ph
www.discoveryhotels-resorts.com

Florentina Homes
L Rovira Rd, Barangay Bantayan, Dumaguete City, Negros Oriental 6200
Tel: (035) 422 4338
florentinahomes@yahoo.com
www.florentinahomes.com

Hoyohoy Villas
Santa Fe, Bantayan Island, Cebu
Tel: (032) 438 9223
info@hoyohoy-villas.com
www.hoyohoy-villas.com

Malapascua Exotic Island Dive and Beach Resort
PO Box 1200, Cebu City 6000
Tel: (032) 406 5428 (Cebu landline); 0917 327 6689 (mobile phone, Malapascua)
info@malapascua.net
www.malapascua.net

Shangri-La's Mactan Resort and Spa
Punta Engano Rd, PO Box 86, Lapu-Lapu City, Cebu 6015
Tel: (032) 231 0288
mac@shangri-la.com
www.shangri-la.com/cebu/mactanresort/

MINDANAO

Caves Dive Resort
Agoho, Mambajao, Camiguin 9100
Tel: (088) 387 0077
cavesresort@yahoo.com
www.cavesdiveresortcamiguin.com

Sagana Resort
Cloud Nine, Siargao Island, Surigao del Norte
Tel: 0919 809 5769 (mobile phone)
sagana@cloud9surf.com
www.cloud9surf.com

Index

Page numbers of illustrations appear in **bold**.

ACKNOWLEDGEMENTS

The author would like to thank the following organisations for their very valuable assistance in making this project possible:

The Philippine Department of Tourism • The Philippine Tourism Promotions Board • Traders Hotel, Manila • Kapuluan Vista Resort, Pagudpud, Ilocos Norte, Luzon • Villa Angela, Vigan, Ilocos Sur, Luzon • Little Surfmaid Resort, San Juan, San Fernando, La Union, Luzon • Island Tropic Hotel, Lucap, Alaminos, Pangasinan, Luzon • The Manor at Camp John Hay, Baguio, Benguet, Luzon • Sagada Homestay, Sagada, Mountain province, Luzon • Banaue Hotel, Banaue, Mountain province • La Laguna Beach Club, Puerto Galera, Mindoro Oriental • Asturias Hotel, Puerto Princesa, Palawan • Ephesians Travel and Tours, Puerto Princesa, Palawan • Lagen Island Resort, El Nido, Palawan • Discovery Shores, Boracay, Aklan, Panay • Shangri-La's Mactan Resort and Spa, Mactan Island, Cebu • Hoyohoy Villas, Santa Fe, Bantayan Island, Cebu • Malapascua Exotic Island Dive and Beach Resort, Malapascua Island, Cebu • Florentina Homes, Dumaguete, Negros Oriental • The Danish Lagoon Restaurant and Beach Resort, San Juan, Siquijor • Anda White Beach Resort, Anda, Bohol • Charts Resort, Alona Beach, Panglao, Bohol • Sagana Resort, Cloud Nine, Siargao Island, Mindanao • Caves Dive Resort, Agoho, Camiguin, Mindanao